Return Date

Staffordsh

THE
MANAGER AS
COMMUNICATOR

THE
MANAGER
AS
COMMUNICATOR
Sandra E. O'Connell, Ph.D.

UNIVERSITY
PRESS OF
AMERICA

LANHAM • NEW YORK • LONDON

University Press of America,® Inc.

4720 Boston Way
Lanham, MD 20706

3 Henrietta Street
London WC2E 8LU England

This edition reprinted in 1986 by University Press of America, Inc.
by arrangement with Harper & Row, Publishers, Inc. New York, New York

Library of Congress Cataloging in Publication Data

O'Connell, Sandra E., 1940-
    The manager as communicator.

    Reprint. Originally published: San Francisco :
Harper & Row, © 1979. (Continuing management education
series)
    Includes bibliographical references and index.
    1. Communication in management.   2. Communication in
personnel management.   I. Title.
[HF5718.03   1986]   658.4'5   86-13170
ISBN 0-8191-5402-4 (pbk. : alk. paper)

All University Press of America books are produced on acid-free
paper which exceeds the minimum standards set by the National
Historical Publications and Records Commission.

For Mary S. McMahon
Manager and Communicator

CONTENTS

PREFACE

Nine years ago I began working with the managers of a large organization, my goal to help them improve their communication skills. I needed material for my program which would be both sound conceptually and practical in presentation. I found, however, only "cookbooks" (*Ten Easy Steps to Good Communication*) or texts that seemed suited to a semester's course of study in a university graduate school. Little of this met my criteria or the managers' needs, so I began developing my own materials, including exercises, case studies, lectures, and self-assessment forms.

The Manager as Communicator is the result of my research and the subsequent development of that program.

This book was written to aid managers and students in face-to-face communication as it relates to management functions. Although memos, reports, manuals, and handbooks are an important form of communication, these writing skills are not covered in this book. I have found that business is usually transacted initially on a face-to-face basis with the printed word supplying documentation, follow-up, and a permanent record. Many books on effective business writing are available for those who wish to improve their written skills.

You'll find help here in handling many management tasks, including getting work done at meetings, giving explanations, conducting performance appraisals, and building open communication. Each chapter includes examples and actual case histories to help you apply what you have read. Throughout the book, self-assessment forms are provided for you to evaluate your own skills and to identify areas for im-

provement. The last chapter deals with ways to change behavior. Here you will be able to bring together the assessments from previous chapters and develop a personal plan for improving your own communication program.

The hundreds of managers I worked with during those nine years gave me a deep insight into the day-by-day communication problems of the modern business. The framework of *The Manager as Communicator* emerged after many workshops and hours of consulting with them in different types of organizations.

Writing is lonely, especially for the person used to face-to-face communication. It was often hard to stay with the task of assembling this material, especially without the feedback I normally get from clients. My colleague, Alan Perry, however, provided that feedback, reading each chapter carefully, even when it came by the poundful. His comments and guidance contributed significantly to the final result. The innumerable drafts and finished manuscript were handled patiently and expertly by Lillian Lee. Fortunately, she read as she typed, and the final product is better because of her work.

My colleagues in both the International Communication Association and the Industrial Communication Council were valuable resources as they help to keep me current on both theory and practice. The people who are my support system have asked about my progress, sympathized, prodded, and encouraged me. As always, my mother provided her own special support. And I shall always be grateful to the many managers who offered me their communication problems. For the solution to those problems was the basis for this book. My thanks to each of you.

The Manager as Communicator offers no formulas or recipes. Human communication is much too varied and complex for easy answers. However, I do provide specific help in the form of suggestions, planning methods, and ways to assess your own communication style and skills. The concepts and their applications are based on a combination of theory, research, and practice.

You may be reading *The Manager as Communicator* for your own information, as part of a management development program, or as a student in a business or communication course. I hope you find the material useful as you seek to improve the quality of your performance and relations with others in the workplace.

Sandra E. O'Connell

THE
MANAGER AS
COMMUNICATOR

CHAPTER 1
MANAGEMENT FUNCTIONS AND THE COMMUNICATION PROCESS

You may be a supervisor, a department manager, a vice president, or a chief executive. Perhaps you supervise five file clerks, direct a production line of 50 people, manage a staff unit, or oversee a million dollar corporation. All of you are managers; your job is to accomplish goals through and with others. Peter Drucker[1] has defined management's responsibilities as contributing to three purposes:

> Fulfilling the specific purpose and mission of the institution
> Making work productive and the worker achieving
> Managing social impacts and social responsibilities

Traditionally, management means performing a number of functions: planning, organizing, staffing, directing, controlling, and innovating. Management texts often discuss communication as a management function. Most organizations acknowledge communication as an important part of the manager's job.

COMMUNICATION IS A PROCESS

This book is based on a different view of the role of communication in management; communication is a management process, not a management function. A process refers to *how* something is done, not what is

---

[1] Peter F. Drucker, *Management: Tasks, Responsibilities, Practices* (New York: Harper & Row, 1973), p. 40.

done. For example, when planning, you gather information, write memos, and then meet with others to explain the plan. Planning is the function; communication is the process used to achieve the function. In order to delegate, you must discuss what needs to be done, how much authority the person has, and then find out how well the delegated tasks were fulfilled. Rather than being a separate function, communication is a process enabling you to carry out management functions.

When communication is seen as a process acting synergistically with other management functions, its place in the manager's job expands. When viewed as only one of many functions, communication becomes a marginal activity, a luxury when time or money is available, but with little direct relationship to organizational outcomes. When communication is viewed as a process, a manager will begin to think more systematically about how communication behavior will affect the other management functions. At first, because it is a new way of looking at your job, the process view of communication involves more work for you as a manager. Once you build communication into your management functions, the results should encourage you, and eventually the process will become easier.

Many managers recognize the importance of communication but have difficulty carrying out their good intentions. They don't have the time, the skills, or the resources to communicate. Effective communication takes time: to plan, to develop needed skills, to carry out, and to review. However, in the long run, appropriate planning and developing communication skills will save time, as anyone who has tried to straighten out a problem resulting from misunderstood instructions will testify.

Limiting Factors

In addition to the problem of time, there are a number of factors limiting communication which are difficult for most managers to influence. These are the parameters in which you must operate.

First is the size of your organization. Although small organizations can suffer from poor communication, problems tend to increase with size. Large organizations inherently produce information overload.[2]

---

[2] W. Charles Redding, *Communication Within the Organization* (New York: Industrial Communication Council, 1972), p. 90.

You have more information than you can absorb, but this does not necessarily mean that you get everything you need or need everything you get. The more you receive, the more sorting out you have to do, and the more perplexing communication becomes. It is impossible for everyone to know everything. As a manager, part of your communication responsibility is to make decisions about who gets to know what and to see that needed information is clearly explained.

As an organization increases in size, the number of levels through which a message must flow also increases. Look at your organization chart and count the number of levels between you and the chief executive. This is equal to the number of levels a message must pass through from the chief executive to reach you. Every link in the human communication chain adds to the likelihood of distortion and information fallout. It is impossible for anyone to completely transfer one person's meaning to another person. Each person adds or deletes details, and changes the messages in subtle or not so subtle ways. The messages which have traveled some distance in the organization may not be very accurate.

Another limiting factor is your own access to information, whatever your position. How much information do you receive? Are you included in a variety of networks? One of the deepest frustrations of supervisors and managers is poor communication from those above them. For example, an organizational change is pending. Rumors are flying, and people are asking if they will be laid off, transferred, or asked to take an early retirement. How well can you answer them if you can't get information from your superiors? Perhaps they do not know the answers or are unwilling to disclose anything until all the decisions have been made. A lack of the needed details has to make your ability to communicate more difficult.

The organization, then, can put limits on your communication by withholding information you need, by not providing resources to support communication, or by establishing a climate of poor communication. Of course, many organizations do not restrict their managers in this way. Some have reasonably open communication from the top and provide needed communication resources.

As difficult as the restrictions may be, you are still responsible for your own communication. The people who work for you rely on you for a critical amount of communication. "I don't have the time," or "It's my boss's fault" are not satisfactory responses for the failure to work at communication. You are the only one responsible for your own behavior.

COMMUNICATION CONCEPTS

The terms "communication," "information," "message," and "communications" are often used interchangeably. Distinctions need to be drawn among these terms, as they do not have the same meaning.

Communication is the process of creating and sharing meanings. I experience an event, have an idea, make an observation, and want to share it with you. I go through a complicated process (that may appear to be easy) to share my meaning with you. In an organization, communication is the flow of these messages through a network of interdependent relationships.[3] The process becomes enormously complex at this point as we take into account the size of the organization and the numbers of people who are included in the communication networks.

Information is best defined as the raw data used to make decisions; it is static, impersonal, logical, nonhuman.[4] It is important to recognize that all information is not necessarily a message. Information becomes a message when it has been perceived and interpreted by someone else. A message, then, is the meaning given to the information by the individual.

Communications are the products or events created to share meaning with others. A newsletter, a staff meeting, the company newspaper, and bulletin boards are all products or events. Communication occurs when people have received some sort of message from the product or event and have placed their own interpretation upon it. Managers often assume that the product or event itself is communication, but this assumption overlooks the distinction between the intended message (contained in the product or event) and the perceived message, which is the result of the total communication process. The perceived message is influenced by a number of factors, such as the networks used, the level of trust, the choice of media, the size of the organization, and so on. Since people act on the basis of what an event means to them, it is vital to remember the distinction between communication and communications. The manager as communicator is a person who takes full account of both communications and communication as each management task is performed.

The people who study language and behavior have helped us to

---

[3] Gerald M. Goldhaber, *Organizational Communication* (Dubuque, IA: Wm. C. Brown, 1974), p. 113.
[4] Gerald M. Goldhaber, Harry S. Dennis, III, Gary M. Richetto, and Osmo A. Wiio, *Information Strategies: New Pathways to Corporate Power* (Englewood Cliffs, N.J.: Prentice-Hall, 1979), p. 19.

understand that the key to communication is the meaning people give to words, not the words themselves.[5] For example, you receive a note stating, "The boss wants to see you." If several people read this, each will have a different response. Some will want to know, "When?"; others will ask, "What's gone wrong now?"; someone else will say, "Wonder what it's all about?" A few will reply, "Good." The response varies because each person has different experiences and so "hears" a different message.

In this example the meaning you impart to the phrase comes from experiences with past bosses, your present boss, teachers, and parents. Each has contributed to the experience bank you bring to the phrase, "The boss wants to see you."

If, instead of reading the words, you saw video tape, your response would vary even more. The tape would add two dimensions missing from print: the boss's voice and body expression. When we refer to language, we are actually referring to three different elements: symbolic language (words); paralanguage (the dynamics of voice); and nonverbal language (physical cues and the use of space).

Symbolic Language

Words are symbols, something we have agreed will stand for something else. Because of the variety of individual experience, each person's words are based on a different point of reference. "No individual ever quite experiences the same environmental stimuli as that person standing near him who seems to be occupying the same time and space . . . human responses will never be predictable by computer."[6] Recognizing the diversity of human experience and the consequent variety of meanings for words is central to becoming an effective communicator. Only common usage and agreement on meaning allow us to use words with any degree of understanding. Many of us have been trained to rely on the dictionary as an arbiter of meaning, but the dictionary is actually a collection of some of the agreed-upon meanings. It does not tell us anything about individual experiences and responses to words. Precision in language—the selection of words which most accurately reflect your experience—is central to effective communication. However, never assume that your meaning is the same as another person's meaning. This

---

[5] Don Fabun, *Communications: The Transfer of Meaning* (New York: Macmillan, 1968), p. 19.
[6] Willard Gaylin, M.D., *Feelings: Our Vital Signs* (New York: Harper & Row, 1979), p. 24.

is especially true when discussing values, opinions, and abstractions. What is most important is to discover if your meaning is anywhere close to the other person's meaning. The selection of words, the symbolic language, is the first step in creating and sharing of meaning.

Paralanguage

Paralanguage includes the dynamics of voice quality: stress on sounds or words, duration of sound, tone, inflection, and pause.[7] From infancy we are sensitive to tone of voice. Long before words, children respond to the soothing sounds of their parents' voices, the cooing of grandparents, and the harsh wail of a brother or sister. As we grow older, we grow more sophisticated in our responses to rising inflections indicating a question, loudness to gain attention, harshness for punishment. Early experiences and the pattern of inflections in different parts of the country condition our responses to this form of language.

Nonverbal Language

Nonverbal language has been divided into two systems: kinesics, or the various body and facial movements; and proxemics, or the use of space. Several popular books suggest that kinesics (which they call "body language") is a formula allowing you to "read a person like an open book." The research suggests that nonverbal language is much too subtle and complex to be a formula.[8] Reading physical cues depends a great deal on the context in which they occur, your culture (Midwestern or Southern, Asian or American) and your past experience with each other. The better we know someone, the more likely we are to "read" the person's kinesic language accurately. Making assumptions about a gesture or facial expression without checking out the meaning can lead to misunderstanding and blocked messages even in the most intimate relationships.

Proxemics is an important part of the communication process in organizations. The size of someone's office, whether or not there is a window and how many, and arrangement of furniture all give messages as to the status and openness of the communicator. It is apparent to most managers that sitting behind a large desk may be a barrier to

---

[7] Joseph A. De Vito, *The Interpersonal Communication Book* (New York: Harper & Row, 1976), p. 359.
[8] Ray L. Birdwhistell, *Kinesics and Context: Essays on Body Motion Communication* (Philadelphia: University of Pennsylvania Press, 1970).

communication. Yet this does not hold true in every situation. It depends on you, the amount of contact you have had in the past, and what you wish to communicate.

In Summary

We simultaneously and automatically take in three sets of language as we attempt to create and share meanings. Research suggests that 50 to 70 percent of meaning in any given message is derived from paralanguage and nonverbal language. This is not to say that words are unimportant, but that it is the particular combination of words, tone, and physical expressiveness that gives us total meaning.

INFORMATION/MESSAGE TYPES

As you review your job functions, you will find you need certain kinds of information to help your unit to perform well. The information is then transformed into various messages for various people. The types of information needed to keep an organization functioning effectively can be divided into four categories as shown in Table 1.1. These four types

TABLE 1.1   Information Types

	Definition	*Examples*
Regulative	Forms of direction and control	Goal statements, planning meetings, one-year plans
Task	Need for completion of specific tasks	Accounting reports, operating procedures, manuals, meetings to solve work problems
Integrative	Feelings for self, peers, the work, and the organization	Orientation, performance appraisal, corporate reports, company newspaper, interaction with supervisor
Innovative	Responding to the environment, processing new ideas, solving problems	Suggestion systems, task forces, subordinate identifying a problem

SOURCE: Table based on categories suggested by Howard Greenbaum, "The Appraisal and Management of Organizational Communication," *Academy of Management Journal*, December 1974.

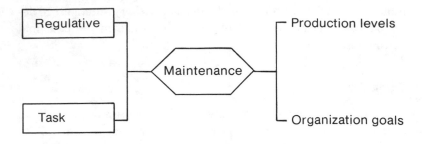

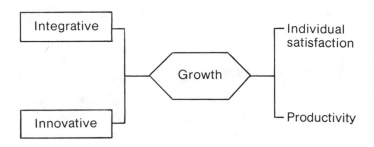

Figure 1.1 Information/message types.

correspond to the two primary organization goals of maintaining the current business, and promoting the growth of individuals and the organization (see Figure 1.1).

Maintenance communication tends to flow from the top down and is therefore more subject to impact from management. Growth communication relies more on an upward flow and is not as systematic as regulative and task. As a manager you can assess the communication needs of your unit by examining each of these information/message systems.

Regulative

How do people find out about the direction of the unit, the policies for achieving goals, and the boundaries which may limit them? Regulative communication enables people to know where they are headed and to direct their energies toward these goals. Without clear, well-communicated goals, effort is expended in the wrong direction; when the boundaries are unknown or fuzzy, mistakes are made, efficiency is lowered, and work may need to be redone. Regulative communication is vital to maintaining the organization, meeting production or service goals, keeping tasks directed toward a goal and within appropriate boundaries. Examples of regulative communication cited previously are often the result of group input and meetings. Chapter 3 covers this information/message type.

Task

Task-related information encompasses a substantial portion of communication in organizations. Closely related to regulative information, but more specific in nature, task communication enables people to do their jobs.

Acquiring and processing of task information is fundamental to any organization. Without it almost nothing happens. In general organizations manage task information reasonably well—at least, better than the other types. After being in an organization for a few months, most people find out what they need to know to do their job. Recent research indicates that people are generally satisfied with communication needed to do the job.[9] The question, of course, is with what degree of efficiency? Could the task be done faster, more accurately, and with less frustration if the flow of task-related information were improved?

The questions for determining this are fairly simple. Is the information you get clear, complete, accurate, and timely? Are the manuals clearly written, up to date, and organized for easy access? How many people do you have to go through for a ruling on an exception? Do you find out about changes which affect your job after they have been made? How clearly are policies, procedures, and technical information explained? This daily communication in the workplace is covered in Chapter 4.

Integrative

Employees get integrative messages in a variety of ways, from the hiring interview and the orientation process, as well as from interactions with co-workers. The organization does much integrative communication for you, most often at the corporate level. The employee handbook, benefits booklets, the employee newspaper, management newsletters, and video tape news shows are some of the ways that

---

[9] Gerald M. Goldhaber, Michael P. Yates, D. Thomas Porter, and Richard Lesniak, "State of the Art, Organizational Communication: 1978," *Human Communication Research*, vol. 5, no. 1, Fall, 1978, p. 82.

organizations communicate integrative information. Through these media people learn what is expected of them and what rewards they will receive.

The corporate communication efforts and interactions on the job and performance appraisals have a cumulative effect; gradually the individual employee develops a sense of being part of the organization. Integration means feeling competent as an individual, having regard for colleagues, and being satisfied with the organization as a good place to work.

Innovative

Innovative communication helps the organization to respond to change, process new ideas from all levels in the organization, and provide a means for continual growth. This information/message type receives the least attention in most organizations.

In order for innovative communication to be successful, a number of factors have to work together. First, members have to perceive that problems are supposed to be aired, and that change is desired. In general people will communicate that which appears to be in their best interests. Criticizing the status quo and identifying problems can be risky for the person trying to move up in the organization. Unless the organization accepts and rewards such behavior, employees will withhold new ideas and perceived problems. If new ideas which are offered simply disappear without a response from the hierarchy, if they are rejected because "we've always done it this way," then employees quickly learn that innovative messages are not really desired and they stop sending them. The organization then becomes error-suppressing. That is, management responds negatively to the identification of problems, making it unrewarding for the next individual who spots a problem.

The cost of turning off innovative messages is high. An organization which is isolated from both problems and new ideas will eventually end up "managing by crisis." When everyone is busy "fighting fires," no one has time to think about how the building could be made fireproof. A poor innovative message system also results in less ability to respond to the business environment. The market changes and another company has the new product, because your sales people who knew the clients' needs could not get their ideas to senior management. Being removed from new ideas is a high price to pay for poor innovative communication. Building open communication—the risks and advantages as well as needed skills—is the subject of Chapter 6.

SUMMARY

The nature of modern organizations places great demands on today's managers. Knowing how the communication process affects management functions provides a different perspective on your job. Increasing your communication skills then becomes an important ingredient of managerial effectiveness.

The four information/message types (regulative, task, integrative, innovative) and the three levels of language (symbolic, para- and non-verbal) are categories to help you spot potential breakdowns in communication. The needs of the organization strongly influence the role of each message. You may, for example, be in a period of rapid expansion where innovation is most important. During budget reduction and strict production schedules, however, regulative is most critical. If your organization has gone through a period of change and is now seeking stability, integrative messages would be emphasized.

Regulative messages have to be present in order for the others to take on meaning. Your life as a manager is not as neat as Table 1.1. Messages shift and flow. Any given conversation may contain all four message types. Explaining is used most often in regulative and task messages, while the more interactive one-to-one communication is required by performance appraisal (integrative) and responding to change (innovative).

The subsequent chapters can help you to identify your communication style and level of effectiveness for getting work done at meetings, giving explanations, conducting performance discussions, and building open communication. Developing a personal communication plan, using the guidelines in Chapter 7, can be a significant step in becoming a manager who is also a communicator.

CHAPTER 2
COMMUNICATION STYLES

Managers seem to be in search of an elusive key which, once possessed, will open the door to all organizational results and individual satisfaction. Yet people and organizations are much too complex for any such key.

I have worked with managers as they conducted staff meetings, gave complicated instructions, struggled with a discipline problem, gathered information for a long-range plan, and encouraged a supervisor to take on more responsibility. What enables one manager to consistently get results *and* maintain satisfying relationships, while others fail to achieve results and alienate their subordinates?

This chapter presents one approach to improving communication through understanding four styles, which can be used in a variety of situations. The communication styles are a framework in which to view your own behavior, and the results you hope to achieve. Before reading this chapter, you may complete the self-assessment sheet on p. 25. Don't complete the scoring until you have read this chapter. The styles are based on the work of Maier [1] and have been developed over time because managers in numerous workshops found them a useful way to understand the effect of their behavior on employees.

The four styles—blaming, telling, selling, and problem solving— are described in Table 2.1. It illustrates what happens in each style ac-

---

[1] Norman R. F. Maier, *The Appraisal Interview: Objectives, Methods, and Skills* (New York: Wiley, 1966).

cording to goal of the communication, type of language used, motivation for change, what happens to feelings, and anticipated results.

BLAMING

Goal

"Who did this?"
"Your reports are always late."
"Why didn't you tell me before the checks went out?"
"You ought to know better than that."

The goal of the blaming style is to find fault or discover someone to blame. The focus is not on solving the problem, but on finding someone to take the blame. At times, a manager does need to discover who was responsible for a particular action. However, this style is accusing, whereas holding someone accountable is more likely to be problem solving. The manager often infers a motive (you did something wrong) rather than describing the problem.

Communication Behavior

Blaming communication behavior is characterized by judgmental language and an accusing tone of voice.

"You have an atrocious attendance record."
"You never pay attention to the new cases."
"Why is your unit the worst in the department?"

In each of these phrases, one word emphatically shifts the meaning to blame. "Atrocious" is loaded with judgment, a negative standard and a comparison with others. The use of "never" in the second example carries an absoluteness which is a sweeping judgment, giving the person no room to explain or engage in a dialogue. "The worst" has the same components: judgment, comparison, and implication one could have done differently. The person who "never pays attention" may have been a trainee, distracted by a new procedure, or under a heavy workload. It may appear, based on some observations, that the clerk "never" pays attention. However, never is an absolute term which, for accuracy's sake, should be used judiciously. Words like "always," "never," or "certainly" tend to close off communication and make it difficult to solve the problem.

Blaming language traps the other person. This trap, sprung early in

TABLE 2.1 Communication Styles

	Blaming	Telling	Selling	Problem Solving
Goal	Find fault Criticize Accuse	Give directions Action to be taken	Provide information Gain acceptance of plan/action	Establish mutual interest Develop actions together
Language	Judgmental language Loaded words Low listening level Defensive Manager does all the talking	Controlling "You will" Manager dominates conversation	Persuasive "Oughta wanna" Attempt to overcome objection Manager encourages other person to talk	Exploring questions Information gathering Sharing of ideas, opinions No one dominates
Feelings	Are denied Hostility generated "You're wrong"	Not listened to Sympathize with, but	Heard but not dealt with "You shouldn't feel that way"	Accepted and explored Used to resolve problem Some sharing by both parties
Motivation	Threat implied or stated Relies on acceptance of judgment	It's policy Threat implied No choice	If person accepts your benefit Personal: "Do it for me"	Results come from focus on the situation rather than on the person Person has had opportunity to influence the outcome

Results	Each party is defensive Others are blamed Action may be taken but not wholeheartedly Resentment and anger carry over to next conversation	Passive acceptance Possible resentment	Action may be short term Active acceptance as long as appeals were appropriate	Action more likely as all views are considered Mutual respect Frustration if person does not have skills or information to participate
When to Use	Hardly ever Risk for defensive and a poor relationship in the future is high If "facts" are most clear When other styles have failed	If required by law or other business restraints If no possibility for change Helpful to supply reasons	If insight and information on appeals are accurate When past problem solving efforts have not worked If you can follow through on the benefits	Recommended style for gaining change in behavior When information from others is needed to resolve problem If relying on other(s) to effectively carry out plan Useful in developing people who will be problem solvers

the conversation, triggers a defensive response which is likely to continue throughout the conversation. Defensiveness nearly always escalates into closed communication from which each party goes a different way feeling "right" and abused by the other. Blaming communication is unlikely to change behavior and is a poor basis for future interactions.[2]

Feelings

The defensiveness generated by the blaming style is most apparent when we look at what happens to people's feelings. Being blamed tends to generate hostility and feelings of being trapped and attacked. People react differently to this feeling: Some will clam up and withdraw; others will be hurt; some will aggressively challenge the blamer.

Whatever feelings are expressed are usually denied by the other person. Often the person doing the blaming wants to keep the situation rational, but does not necessarily behave that way. The usual response is:

"Let's keep feelings out of this. Just deal with the facts."

A blaming style, has already brought feelings into the situation: anger, resentment, and need to blame someone or to hold them up to ridicule. Yet the manager may try to reduce the employee's feelings to irrelevancy. In other words, it's all right for the manager to be angry, but not for the employee to feel resentful and attacked. The imbalance between manager and subordinate in expressing feelings, and the attempt to act as if feelings were not a part of behavior both contribute to "closed" communication. Feelings are part of everyone's behavior; ignoring them prevents two people from dealing realistically with each other.

Motivation

"Why should this person change?"

This question is central to much of a manager's communication. The basis of change in the blaming style is power. There is a threat, direct ("Do this or you're fired") or indirect ("We'll talk about your promotion when this is corrected").

---

[2] Jack R. Gibb, "Defensive Communication," *The Journal of Communication*, Vol. 11, No. 3, September 1961, pp. 141–148.

In order for the motivation to be effective, the person must: (1) accept the manager's judgment, (2) not wish to sustain a loss in status, pay, or responsibility, and (3) feel certain that the threat will be carried out. If these factors are not present, the motivating forces are greatly weakened. More importantly, motivation by threat is not an adult way of treating another person. Change is particularly difficult if the person does not perceive the action to be in his or her best interests.

Results

What can you expect to happen as a result of blaming communication?

1. The person *may* accept the blame, acknowledge your judgment, and behave according to your wishes. This acceptance may also bring resentment, apprehension, and other negative feelings.
2. Others are blamed. The most typical reaction to being blamed is to blame someone or something else. The reason for the failure in performance is now the other department which didn't do its work on time; a failure in the computer system, a peer, or even the manager who did not give clear instructions. Think of the times you may have reacted defensively and you will realize the inevitability of this response. The conversation seldom resolves anything.
3. Action can be taken with great reluctance and often with severe consequences for future relationships. The trust level is impaired, and further communication becomes difficult.

Obviously, the blaming style is not recommended. It is included in the discussion of style for several reasons. First, managers often use it, unaware of the responses they are triggering. Second, some managers feel a "strong offense" is best in dealing with others; that offense often takes the form of blaming others.

This discussion demonstrates that the results of blaming seldom warrants its use. Holding people accountable for performance and their responsibilities is central to effective management, and I do not mean that you let problems or mistakes slip by you because blaming others is not effective. The word style is important; how you go about describing the problem is related to the results you achieve. The remaining styles provide more options and will enable you to give negative feedback without touching off defensive reactions while still treating your employees in an adult manner.

TELLING

Goal

A manager using the telling style gives directions, defines action to be taken, and anticipates solutions. The purpose is to have others do precisely what you want them to do. Two-way discussion is minimal; the manager does most of the talking. In addition, there is an element of "you will"; i.e., the course of action has been decided—carry it out.

Communication Behavior

The amount of time used by each person is a clue in each style. When telling, the manager is dominant, doing 80-100 percent of the talking. The language is often clear and precise, especially if it is task-oriented. In addition the language has a finality about it—"you will" is implied or stated. This style is often seen in implementing new procedures, following safety instructions, or instructing a trainee in the elements of a prescribed task.

Feelings

Feelings are not allowed much expression in this style. The absoluteness of the instructions leaves little room for them. If feelings are expressed, they may be sympathized with, but no more.

"I know this procedure means undoing all of last week's quotes, but. . . ."

"It may be hard for you to understand why we are doing this, but. . . ." The use of "but" is the tip-off. The feelings are mildly acknowledged, then dismissed.

Motivation

The primary stimulus for action lies in the apparent lack of choice. The new procedure may have been decided upon at a higher level, such as when a safety requirement is dictated by the Occupational Safety and Health Administration; the person expected to carry this out is really given no option. This style works most effectively when both parties understand there really is no choice. Where alternatives exist and the manager imposes one over the other, the employee may have difficulty in accepting direction.

For example, with a tardiness problem, a manager may direct someone to take a different train or get up earlier without any discussion of the reasons for lateness. The alternative the manager selects may not be the best for the situation. Even if it is, a manager is imposing actions for which the individual should be responsible. The chances of success are increased by explaining reasons so the employee at least may recognize the rationale governing the directive.

Results

Achieving positive results with the telling style depends a great deal on using it appropriately. When everyone understands the limits of the situation, telling can be effective. However, when the circumstances are ambiguous, telling creates resentment which can surface later. Acceptance often occurs because of the apparent lack of choice. The person may say (or think), "O.K., if you want it that way." This attitude can lead to subtle sabotage of your program, if only to show you how wrong you were.

Use

The selection of this style depends on a good analysis of the constraints of the situation and the people involved. It is most useful in matters of health, safety, taxes, and government regulation, or when policies and procedures have already been decided upon. Selecting the telling style does not exclude explaining why something is being done.

SELLING

Goal

> You want five people to work overtime; you explain the reasons for the backlog and then seek acceptance of your plan.
> You want a work unit's monthly production level increased; you let its members know what they are doing, what the job standards are, and the advantages to them of improving.

Selling has two primary goals: to provide information and then to gain acceptance of a plan or action. The manager who is "selling" employees is persuasive and trying to be convincing. This manager has results in mind and knows how to achieve them.

Communication Behavior

As with other selling, this communication is essentially persuasive: establishing needs and motives for a person to do what you want. As a manager, the "product" you are selling is completed work schedules, taking on new responsibilities, or serving on a task force.

The language of persuasion is characterized by the implication that you know the best alternative. In their discussion of performance problems, Mager and Pipe[3] call this "You really oughta wanna. . . ." They outline a number of alternatives to exhortation in solving performance problems.

In selling, appeals which are assumed to be motivating are described to the other person. The communication also relies on anticipating and overcoming objections. The manager still dominates in this style, but in contrast with telling, listens more to discover the impact of the appeals and to hear objections.

Selling people on your ideas has long been recognized as an asset in business. As a technique of managing people, it has limitations. This style assumes that you know best, have the "right" answer, and have predicted accurately what would appeal to each individual, which is a rather large assumption even for an experienced manager. Again, it is difficult for people to accept what they feel is not in their best interests.

Feelings

Good salespeople recognize that understanding and responding to feelings are important in closing the sale. In the selling style, feelings are not closed off or ignored. They are dealt with by being heard and acknowledged, but are not really a part of the discussion. A persuasive manager indicates that the person ought not to have the feelings. The long-service employee who is being moved to a different unit may feel the company is overlooking experience and loyalty. The persuader will acknowledge it is a disturbing situation, then attempt to neutralize the feelings with, "You shouldn't feel that way. The company has gone to a lot of trouble to find you this job." The appearance of responding to feelings is there, but not the substance. The manager is, in effect, saying, "You are wrong to have these feelings." Such behavior robs the individual of legitimate feelings and reduces the basis for understanding.

---

[3] Robert F. Mager and Peter Pipe, *Analyzing Performance Problems or "You Really Oughta Wanna"* (Belmont, CA: Fearon • Pitman, 1970).

Motivation

If you are exceptionally good at determining what appeals to other people, you can be successful with this style. The stimulus for change relies on acceptance of the appeals. If you are dangling a promotion in front of a person who prefers to be a technical expert, you probably won't succeed. For the appeals to be appropriate, you must have accurately assessed the person and the situation. Further, you must be able to back up your appeals with action. If the person is not allowed to go to the training class, or does not receive the raise, your credibility is damaged and future communication will be suspect. The most important appeal is what the individual feels is in his or her best interests.

PROBLEM SOLVING

Goal

> "I see from the monthly service report that 15 percent of the complaints have not been answered."
> "The production sheets show we are 5 percent behind last month's production."
> "Last week I heard you speak in an abrupt tone to two technicians."

The goal of problem solving is for both parties to identify their stake in the problem and to develop a mutually acceptable plan. What distinguishes the problem solving goal from the other styles is descriptive language which builds two-way conversation, particularly at the goal stage.

Communication Behavior

The problem solving style is characterized by questions and descriptive language. Questions are used to seek information, probe feelings and discover other points of view. The communication focuses initially on a search for information, a complete review of the data. The language is nonjudgmental, free of values and loaded words. In this way the other person feels free to express a divergent point of view, to express feelings and to raise questions. The amount of time spent talking and listening is equally balanced between the two people.

Feelings

Problem solving makes feelings part of the data. They are explored and often used to help develop a solution. In addition, feelings are shared, not in a placating way, but with openness and honesty. As a manager, you may share a similar experience or simply state a reaction. The employee may say, "I feel dead-ended in this job." In selling, you might acknowledge you heard it and say, "You really shouldn't feel that way." In problem solving, you may say, "I wasn't aware of that. Tell me what happens to make you feel that way," or "I have felt that way in some jobs myself and found it difficult to change." Feelings are not ignored or criticized in problem solving but dealt with openly as an important basis of behavior.

Motivation

The individual's recognition of the problem and stake in the solution are central to the motivation to change. The forces for change come from within the person, rather than being imposed by the manager. Management literature has demonstrated repeatedly that change is most likely when people have some say in what affects their jobs.[4] The problem solving style relies on understanding each other's motives rather than attacking (blaming), assuming (telling), or persuading (selling).

Use

Problem solving is essentially two adults talking with mutual respect. Because of its participatory nature and high potential for motivation, problem solving is a recommended style; but not without some cautions. First, due to the interest in participative management, some people use problem solving techniques to give the "feeling" of participation when, in fact, a decision has already been made. Or, more likely, the input will not actually have a significant bearing on the decision. Such a tactic is blatantly dishonest as well as counterproductive. Playing at problem solving damages credibility for future interactions and makes people angry. Use problem solving only where the employee will have some influence on the outcome, and be sure that the employee understands the nature and extent of that influence.

The second caution is that some people will have difficulty responding to this style. Problem solving behaviors can be learned, but

---

[4] W. Charles Redding, *Communication Within the Organization* (New York: Industrial Communication Council, 1972) pp. 154–250.

need reinforcement to survive. Perhaps no one ever honestly asked this person's opinion before. Autocratic managers tend to tell people answers to everything, which effectively squelches problem solving abilities. The individual may feel threatened by not having answers to your questions or uncomfortable giving opinions. Patience and *repeated* conversations can help to develop a problem solver. You may have to determine, however, how much time and energy you can put into this process. More people have the capacity to be problem solvers than we realize, but you may discover situations where this isn't true and make use of the other styles.

The benefits of problem solving communication are high: better solutions, increased long-term action, more openness and respect, and more autonomy for the employee. As with most behavior which yields high payoffs, problem solving communication requires skill, concentration, and continued effort on your part.

SUMMARY

The four communication styles form a continuum; you can move in degrees from open problem solving to blaming. You may find that you change styles within the same conversation. The issue here is one of choice; you need to be aware of your own behavior and its consequences.

The styles are not offered as categories in which you peg yourself and others, only as a guide to understanding your own communication. Listen to yourself to identify which style you use most frequently. What percentage of the time are you talking? listening? What questions are you asking? Is your language judgmental? How do you respond to expression of feelings? Once you know the style you are using you can ask whether it is appropriate for the person and the situation, whether it is the most honest and credible choice.

Your desired choice depends on the situational analysis; actual behavior depends on your communication skills. To start out problem solving, a manager asked, "Why did you wait so long to tell me about the equipment problems?" This was well intentioned, but the evaluative language and the attack implied by tone of voice set off defensiveness. A more meaningful question would have been, "What figures do you have on the equipment breakdown?" After some data gathering, the next question would be, "How do you decide when to report malfunctions?" These questions progress to describe the problem in clear terms and then to solutions. The ability to hear yourself and try new behavior is central to choosing a communication style.

pertoire of communication behaviors enables you to respond to
..riety of situations and people. Most of us have a dominant style,
built by personal experience and reinforced by organizational norms.
Using the same approach to every situation ignores the complexity of
people and organizations, and it is self-limiting.

You can widen your communication repertoire by examining your
motives, practicing the needed skills, and listening to yourself.

SELF-ASSESSMENT

Most of us have a dominant communication style. Use the Communication Style Self-Assessment Sheet to determine your style. Then use the
scoring sheet that follows to interpret your style.

SELF-ASSESSMENT OF COMMUNICATION STYLE

Indicate the degree to which you do the following: (You might ask others to fill it out as well.)

	Very Little	Little	Some	Great	Very Great
1. Make judgments early in the conversation.					
2. Share my feelings with others.					
3. Talk about the issues.					
4. Have analyzed others' motives.					
5. Talk about the person.					
6. Use clear and precise language.					
7. Decide on the action before the conversation.					
8. Encourage the other person to discuss feelings.					
9. Am open for new information.					
10. Ask questions which seek agreement with me.					
11. Talk the majority of the time.					
12. Ask questions which get others to describe events.					
13. Talk half the time or less.					
14. Others defend their position to me.					

Scoring Sheet

Item No.	Score	
1	_____	
2		_____
3		_____
4	_____	
5	_____	
6		_____
7	_____	
8		_____
9		_____
10	_____	
11	_____	
12		_____
13		_____
14	_____	
Totals	_____	_____

Total column 1   _____
Total column 2   _____

Interpretation of scores:
very little = 1 point, little = 2 points, some = 3 points, great = 4 points, and very great = 5 points

Interpretation of Communication Style Scores

The most important styles are blaming and problem solving. If you tend to blame, you have a high risk of closed, ineffective communication. If you are a problem solver, you are more likely to have open, effective communication. Each of us encounters circumstances in which we need to tell or sell. However, it is unlikely that a blamer will very often sell, or that a problem solver will use the telling mode unless absolutely necessary.

If your scores in column 1 were 21–28, you are probably a moderate blamer. If these scores were 29–35, you had best examine the people around you and the results of your communication as you are functioning as a strong blamer.

If your scores in column 2 were 21–28, you have a moderate degree of problem solving skills and probably use them judiciously. If your scores are 29–35, you are likely to use problem solving as your dominant style. You may want to examine whether you are always using it appropriately—i.e., are there times when there are no alternatives and telling may be more honest?

CHAPTER 3
GETTING WORK DONE
AT MEETINGS

How much of your time during the last week was spent at meetings? 0–25 percent? 26–50 percent? 51–75 percent? 76–100 percent?

Your answer to this question depends upon your position in the organization; i.e., the higher you go, the more likely you are to spend time in meetings. Managers often find meetings unproductive, a waste of time, and frustrating. Many have come to the conclusion that meetings per se are the culprit, that there is something inherently ineffective about people working in groups.

RATIONALE FOR MEETING SKILLS

This view overlooks the realities of work in modern organizations and blames the product rather than the people who produced it. Complexity and interdependence are two central facts of life in organizations today. Modern technology and the size of many profit and nonprofit institutions makes it virtually impossible for any one person to possess the information, the experience, or the specialized training needed to solve most business problems.

To determine where a new plant should be located, a number of specialists are needed: real estate, construction, transportation, environmental, personnel, tax, and Equal Employment Opportunity. Adopting a new product line calls for a similar number of experts to coordinate the information: marketing, research, product management, packaging, and manufacturing. For a hospital to open a new clinic, many services must be brought together: medical, nursing, social welfare, laboratory, ambulatory care, and administration. Appointing committees and task forces seems to be endemic to organizations.

> The tendency (of the organization) to do more and more work through committees and task forces puts an additional pressure on managers. They were on committees to work on transportation, packaging, training, corporate relocation, minority relations, or to solve particular problems. The immediate response to any problem in the corporation was to form a committee, and managers were likely to get an announcement in the mail that they were appointed to one.[1]

Regulative Communication and Meetings

The types of regulative communication described in Chapter 1 (goals, policies, and manuals) are frequently initiated at meetings. Determining a new product line, doing a five-year human resources plan, identifying a city's recreation needs, figuring the salary program for the next year; all of these decisions will involve a number of specialists and some meetings. Day-to-day task-related problems are another frequent reason for meetings.

Five underlying factors necessitate people getting together in groups. First, as we have seen, the complexity and interdependence of work means it is difficult for any one person to have the knowledge to make decisions and solve problems. Second, the number of people affected makes the costs of decisions so high that the best information is needed, as decisions are not easily reversed. Third, the regulatory environment puts constraints on which, and how, things can be done. Lawyers, industrial relations managers, or tax specialists are often needed to define and analyze the government's requirements. Fourth, power is often concentrated in large organizations, and support is needed to carry out actions, decisions, and policies. Meetings often are used to gain that support. Last, meetings can help to prevent unnecessary conflict and competition from special interests that could undercut or compete with the decision.

There seems to be no way, then, to escape meetings as a fact of organizational life. Yet most organizations do not coach and train managers in the skills needed to perform a significant component of their job.

---

[1] Rosabeth Moss Kanter, *Men and Women of the Corporation* (New York: Basic Books, 1977), p. 64.

Some argue that committees are ineffective because the group is free from individual responsibility. Problems in accountability can occur when groups make decisions, but to transfer that responsibility to one person who cannot possibly process the information needed for decisions is a serious mistake.

How should a company which has experienced rapid expansion be structured?

Where are the future markets for your product?

What services will people need from banks in twenty years?

How will transportation in the cities be managed?

What can be done to reduce this year's operating costs?

Who is available in the organization for top management positions?

What steps can you take to reduce pollution in chemical plants?

What is the role of your government agency under a new administration?

All these questions are examples of issues which need to be addressed by more than one person; many people will be affected by the outcome, and the costs and potential changes can have enormous impact on the organization. Meetings, then, are not an extra duty, but more and more a part of the manager's job.

This chapter presents material which you can adapt as either a leader or a participant. The four topics covered include planning the meeting, behaviors needed during the meeting, leadership style, and postmeeting activities. Within each topic specific behavior is described and suggestions are given which you can use to improve the quality of meetings. A self-assessment form is included at the end of the chapter.

BARRIERS TO EFFECTIVE MEETINGS

Managers have identified a variety of reasons why meetings don't go well.

There is no agenda, or the agenda is not followed.

People don't listen.

Individual goals supersede group goals.

There is no obvious leader.

The leader is not effective in controlling the group.

Meetings run too long.

There is no spirit of compromise.

Extraneous ideas are permitted to intrude.

People don't prepare or haven't done their "homework."
The meetings don't start on time.
People feel intimidated by the status of others.
There are too many interruptions.
The leader can't resolve individual differences.
The right people aren't there.
One or two people monopolize the time.
The goal of the meeting isn't clear.

Not all these problems can be solved by a person with good meeting skills, but many of them can be reduced or eliminated. Three primary approaches are available to you to manage the difficulties which seem to plague meetings in organizations: planning, monitoring your behavior during the meeting, and postmeeting follow-up. You probably call meetings and attend meetings called by others. Planning is critical to the meetings you call, and you can also plan for the meetings you attend.

Most functions in an organization—budget, production schedules, sales, research—are planned. Meetings consume a great deal of time and expense, but often are not planned. The cost factor for meetings can be analyzed by answering the following questions.

How many people were there?
How long did the meeting take?
What was the quality of the decision or outcome: low, mediocre, high?
How many people will be affected by what you did at the meeting?
What is the hourly rate of the people who attended the meeting?
How much did the meeting cost (number of people × hourly rate)?

Given how much the meeting cost, the quality of the decision, and the number of people affected by the outcome, was the time worth it? Was it cost-effective? This is not to suggest that eliminating meetings is a cost-saving step. Often this cannot and should not be done for the reasons discussed earlier. And in the long run, it won't be cost-effective if others have difficulty accepting and implementing decisions. Rather this analysis suggests that you value everyone's time, including your own, enough to get the best results. You can do that by planning, being aware of behaviors needed to help groups function, and doing follow-up after each meeting.

PLANNING ACTIVITIES[2]

The first step is to determine whether or not you need a meeting at all. Even though the complexity and interdependence of most organizations require a significant degree of cooperation and collaboration, not *every* situation calls for a meeting. You can decide whether or not a meeting is needed by answering the following questions:

1. How important is the quality of the decision?
2. Do you possess enough information and expertise to make a high-quality decision?
3. To what degree do others, taken as a group, possess information needed to make the decision?
4. If you make the decision alone, will it be accepted and carried out by others?
5. Will others be motivated to carry out the decision or policy?
6. To what extent are people likely to be in disagreement over the solution to the problem?
7. How important to effective implementation is acceptance of or commitment to the decision?[3]

These questions apply primarily to decision-making situations. There are, of course, many other occasions which call for meetings. These occasions can include updating on projects, explaining procedures, discussing policy, or announcing organizational change. In these cases it is often more efficient to get people together to tell them the same information at the same time, and you may want the group to hear each other's questions and responses. But it is not a time for redoing a decision that has already been made.

Identify the Goal

Knowing the purpose of the meeting is the first and most critical step in planning, as the other planning steps all depend on it. The goal of the meeting should be stated in specific terms so that you can measure progress during the meeting as well as assess effectiveness when it's over. The most common mistake at this point in planning is to state a

---

[2] Material developed with Sara Barnhardt, Ph.D.
[3] Victor H. Vroom and Philip Yetton, "A Normative Model of Leadership Style," in *Readings in Managerial Psychology*, Harold J. Leavitt and Louis R. Pondy, eds. (Chicago: University of Chicago Press, 1973), p. 421.

topic but not the purpose. Below are topics which could necessitate a meeting:

Status of projects
Manual procedures which will be computerized
Training needs
Labor grievance
Workflow
New product or service
Departmental budget
Reorganizing

All these are topics in search of a purpose; each could have more than one purpose, depending on the situation, as illustrated below.

Topic	*Purpose*
Discuss this year's budget.	Outline budget assumptions. Determine major expenses expected for each division. Discover ways to reduce expenses in last quarter.
Review customer service problems.	Identify sources of customer complaints by type of product or service. Evaluate progress made on customer service plan implemented last quarter. Develop strategy to get feedback to manufacturing on problems.

You may have more than one goal or reason for having a meeting on any given topic; be sure that you state what specific outcome or outcomes are expected. Several goals may necessitate more than one meeting. Clarifying and clearly stating the goal contributes to the next steps in planning: who to invite, the amount of time needed, the information required, the agenda, and communication about the meeting. Participants need to know why they were asked and what to expect during the meeting.

Who Should Attend

With the goal in mind, identify the people who should attend the meeting. Since you do not have the information or expertise to deal with the situation alone, who does? If you are looking for acceptance and commitment, who are the people who could be affected by the outcome? It is best to have only the people attend who can directly contribute to the outcome, but organizational life often requires that people be asked for political reasons. Reinforcing this norm will not contribute to the effectiveness of your meetings. If you find yourself frequently inviting people for purely political motives and not for their ability to contribute, ask how clear you are about the purpose of the group and about your own authority.

People are often asked to meetings because of their status or power to make decisions and supply needed resources. Some of these people may or may not be helpful to the meeting itself. One question to ask is, "Who needs to be invited who may *not* be helpful?" The vice president of manufacturing may be defensive about production problems, but is needed for workable solutions. Some managers do not like anything to go on without their personal participation; they may not trust subordinates. These are organizational realities with which you must work. You can handle the necessary attendance of "political" invitees diplomatically by clearly stating the meeting's goal, suggesting who should attend, and offering to keep the manager informed of the group's progress. If done in a memo, follow up with a phone call, making it clear you will report back if the manager chooses not to attend. Many people are overburdened with meetings and some will welcome a well-stated option.

Size

Research over the last 30 years has shown that for problem-solving, small groups of five to seven participants are best. The group can be expanded to nine or ten; once you have 11 or more people, the dynamics change markedly.[4] In larger groups less time is available for each person to comment, the likelihood of factions or subgroups increases, some people are less willing to speak up, and it is harder for the person who called the meeting to manage the conversation and the agenda.

The situation often determines how many people will attend.

---

[4] Dorwin Cartwright and Alvin Zander, *Group Dynamics: Research and Theory* (New York: Harper & Row, 1968, p. 499.

When announcements are made or procedures explained (information-giving), larger groups are quite acceptable. If, however, you want people to ask questions, generally the larger the group, the fewer the questions. When the purpose is information-sharing (status reporting), it is best to keep the group small. Updating can be boring if the other projects have little or no effect on the other participants in the meeting. Staff groups often complain that their meetings are "show 'n' tell," with people vying to demonstrate how well they have done that week. There is little interaction or reason for the group to be together. If you hold meetings like this, ask yourself if you can get the information in another way and use the group's time more productively by identifying interests, problems, or questions appropriate for the entire group.

Physical Arrangements

We often pay little attention to the impact of the physical environment on our behavior, unless that environment makes us quite uncomfortable. Physical arrangements for a meeting are a subtle, but crucial, aspect of planning. You may not have much choice. Monday morning staff meetings are held in your office with a few chairs added. Not every organization has well-furnished conference rooms, and if you do, it may be hard to schedule time in them. A few guidelines are in order:

1. Find a room where chairs and tables can be arranged so that people can easily see and hear each other. Long narrow tables or a classroom set-up are distracting to communication.
2. Try to match the size of the room to the size of the group. A room seating 40 can be overwhelming to a group of six.
3. Be sure you have needed equipment, visual aids, and space to place them if they are needed.
4. Seek comfort wherever possible, in chairs, ventilation, lighting. But large, overstuffed chairs are not conducive to concentration.

An attractive room with an easel and a good conference table will not in itself make your meeting a success, but poor physical arrangements can hurt the best of meetings.

Identify Necessary Information

To achieve your goal, you will need a variety of information. Who knows what you need to know? Who has had similar experience with this kind of situation? What reports or records exist which may be useful? Although the specifics may be unique, you may not be the first to face this problem, so someone could have experience which can be helpful to you. Identify what information will be useful before or during the meeting. Prepare it so that it can be easily and quickly digested, using highlights, summaries, and charts wherever possible. Beware of sending lengthy memos or reports to people in advance. Most often they won't read them, and it can be distracting during the meeting to have people shuffling through papers. Some examples of information requirements are as follows:

Purpose of Meeting	*Information*
Reduce expenses during last quarter.	Last year's budget overruns by division Expense summaries for this year Current projections
Develop staffing requirements for a new plant.	Staffing of a similar plant EEO data for your organization Types of jobs Market surveys for salary in that location
Resolve work distribution which is uneven and results in bottlenecks and delay.	Total amount of work processed by month/quarter Standards of production by each type of job or product Current methods for distributing work Report of another department which solved a similar problem

Invitations to the Meeting

How and when people receive notice of a meeting can influence their participation and the eventual outcome. If you are getting a new group together, you may want to call them to discuss the goals and reasons why you want each person to attend. If you write a memo, be sure to state the goals and time requirements clearly. If someone other than yourself is arranging the meeting (a secretary or administrative assistant), be sure you communicate the goals so that he or she can answer questions when participants are invited. Have some means of determining whether or not people will attend, and let them know if it's all right to send a representative. Time can be wasted if several people aren't there and work has to be redone.

Steps to Achieve the Goal

Given what you want to accomplish, what are the major points or topics that need to be discussed? Review and outline the blocks of material that the group needs to cover. Where do you want to start? With a review of past experience? Stating the problem as it currently appears? Indicating what the outcome needs to be? Where you start depends largely on the history of the group (if it has met before) and the nature of the problem. A detailed outline on problem solving appears at the end of this chapter. You may want to refer to it to determine the major topics for your meeting. In summary, the main points are:

Defining the nature of the problem
Analyzing the cause(s) of the problem
Criteria for acceptable solutions
Available solutions
Selection of best solution
Plan for implementation

Depending on what has occurred before, you may start at any point in the outline. The problem may have already been defined and causes determined and the job of your committee is to come up with solutions. Or you may be trying to figure out what the problem is. Within each main step of the problem solving outline, there are a number of subpoints which you can follow to draft an agenda.

Agenda

Using this draft, develop an agenda showing the sequence of issues and how much time will be spent on each. The problem solving outline and the nature of the issues should suggest a certain order. But there are considerations other than the logic of the issues in developing an agenda. You may not want to take the most controversial item first if you feel it would polarize the group too early, although taking on tough issues early when people are fresh (especially if it will be a long meeting) may be more effective. Once again, as with other aspects of communication, there are no formulas. Use your knowledge of the individuals, how they react to each other in a group setting, the goals, and the available time as guidelines.

Some groups are quite informal and do not need a written agenda, while others have advance agendas and minutes. Handing out an agenda may be of great help in keeping the group on track, but whether or not you distribute an agenda, the issues and available time should be structured. One useful technique is to put the agenda, in outline form, on a flip chart so everyone can see what has to be done. This can serve as a gentle reminder to those who tend to wander off the track, and help you to guide the group to the next topic. Even if you don't use a written or visual agenda, at least give an overview to the group before you begin.

BEHAVIORS NEEDED DURING THE MEETING

You may have noticed that the term "leader" has not been used so far in this chapter. Yet it is common to begin talking about meetings with the concept of leadership. Leadership style is addressed in the next section because first we should establish what behaviors are needed at meetings. The tendency to blame the leader for a group which is not productive absolves the members of responsibility for what happens within the group. Although the leader's role can be critical, especially in structured situations in large organizations, it is often overestimated. Members can, without threatening the position of the leader, behave in ways which are useful to the group. If you are the "leader" of a meeting, you may assume responsibility for things that the group may well be able to do for itself. In so doing, you are limiting the individual members' capacity to function well on their own.

Rather than focus on who does what, we need to think instead of what the members (as a group) need to accomplish. This view of leadership focuses on what functions are needed for the group to reach its goals. Groups need two primary sets of behavior to work effectively: (1) getting the job or task done—task maintenance; and (2) keeping the group in good working order by focusing on *how* they are functioning—group maintenance.

The seven task maintenance behaviors are initiating procedures, giving information or opinions, seeking information or opinions, making assignments and giving directions, clarifying and elaborating, summarizing and evaluating, and consensus testing. The six group maintenance behaviors are encouraging participation, gatekeeping (monitoring flow of communication), reducing tension, clarifying communication, compromising, and managing differences. Each of these has specific effects on members' willingness and ability to carry out needed task behaviors. A group needs all of these functions if it is to be productive and satisfying to members.

At the beginning of a group's work, goal statement and inquiry are much needed. Later, as solutions are proposed, critical testing and compromising may assume more importance. Supporting and encouraging functions are needed all along, but especially as the group moves toward final decisions. Group work will be effective, then, to the degree task and maintenance functions are supplied by members at the appropriate time.

When functions needed by the group are missing, progress is slow and uneven, frustration builds, and the task may not be completed. If members do not sense or cannot provide what is needed (a summary, for example), it is unlikely that group goals will be met. The key task and maintenance functions can be handled almost completely by one person or by different group members. Whichever approach is taken, people must know *why, when,* and *how* to contribute a particular function. Most managers are inexperienced in recognizing the need for group maintenance functions. This is one reason for the poor productivity and feelings of dissatisfaction with many meetings. The effective group member or leader is aware of the types of contributions being made and is able when necessary to provide those which are missing.

Task Behaviors

The seven task behaviors all contribute to getting the job done. Each is used at different times to accomplish the work. The role that each plays will depend upon the purpose of the meeting, the stage of discussion, and the nature of the problem. The ability to use each appropriately can greatly increase the productivity of meetings. For example, when everyone shares a common knowledge of the issues, question asking is more important than information giving.

Initiating Procedures   Early in any meeting, someone needs to propose procedures for how the group will work. This proposal may take the form of defining the problem, stating tasks or goals, and suggesting ways to work on the issues. The leader may often help a group by proposing procedures, but the group should have some opportunity to decide how to tackle the task. At the procedure stage, the limits of the group—amount of time, degree of authority, and resources available—need to be specified. Imposing procedures too early can create difficulties and resentment which are hard to overcome. Knowing the group and the problem are important in determining the timing of this particular task maintenance function. Here are some examples:

> "I thought we could begin by hearing a two-minute report from each person on the project."
> "Should we work on this as an entire group or divide into subcommittees?"
> "What is the best way to tackle this issue?"
> "Let's first review the results chronologically, then by product line, and third by territory. Then we can open up for questions."

Each of these statements gives the group a way to begin working. In some cases, the initiation is really asking the group which is the best way to proceed. A great deal of time is lost and frustration builds when procedures are neither initiated nor adopted.

Giving Information or Opinions   Contributing information and ideas is something most people do without much prodding. There are some exceptions, such as those who need encouragement to speak up, but finding people to talk is not usually difficult. The problem is more likely to be how to control the amount and direction of the conversation. Before reaching any conclusion, a group should first ask, "What do we have to go on?" "How do we know this is a problem?" "What has happened so far?" So individuals offer facts, their own views, interpretation of information, experience, personal values, and hopes. Since this behavior is so common, every manager should be particularly skilled at giving information and opinions.

This means learning how to be brief; generally comments should last only a minute or two. A meeting is not the place to give a speech, and comments should be limited to one key idea. When you get the floor it is tempting to spill out every point you've wanted to make for the last half-hour. Covering several issues at once will confuse and sidetrack the meeting, so discussion should take place on an orderly basis. Make your point briefly when the topic arises. Check yourself for relevance. One of the most frequent complaints about meetings is people who wander off the track. (See the discussion of self-oriented behaviors, below.)

How free do you feel to give information or your opinion at a meeting? If you tend to be reticent, a review of your behavior and feelings about groups appears to be in order. There are numerous reasons why people are quiet in the presence of others. Some are:

Anxiety about position in the group
Lack of clarity about the goals
Fear of being wrong in front of others
Sense of not being able to express oneself

Each of us will have one or more of these feelings in some situations; they are quite realistic. If, however, these feelings frequently keep you from participating, you need to examine their basis. Don't be too quick to denigrate your own contribution, and thus keep it from the group. Although most managers could do with some monitoring to reduce tangents, others need to take more risks in making a contribution.

All groups need people who are good listeners, but as with other behaviors, that task should be shared by group members. Balance your silence with some participation. Planning should be useful to you in seeing where and how you can make contributions.

Seeking Information or Opinions   A characteristic of good problem solvers is that they know what questions to ask, not that they have all the answers. Framing a question in such a way as to get a new view on the problem, to get a contribution from a person who hasn't spoken, asking why instead of accepting conclusions has great impact on the outcome of the task. At meetings you will need direct, open, and clarifying questions. (See Chapter 5 for material on how to frame questions.) Loaded questions may get asked, but they do not contribute much to trust, honesty, or the ability of members to get complete, accurate information.

Questions are sometimes used to give an appearance of inquiry so that people have the "feeling of participation." The best way to achieve participation is to encourage people to talk to each other. If your questions are only a guise and the answers have already been determined, you are wasting your time and that of the other people. Furthermore the dishonesty will only contribute to a lack of credibility which will make it difficult to get anything done.

Clarifying and Elaborating   Clarifying means clearing up confusions (not adding to them), defining terms which have been used in different ways, and indicating where more information is needed. When the eight members of your task force represent different departments, it is likely that a lot of clarifying will be needed to help people under stand each other.

Elaborating involves giving an example, detailed illustration, or reinforcing the point with your own experience. A common but ineffective way that people attempt to clarify is, "I think what Gerry was really trying to say is. . . ." Most of us resent others putting words in our mouths or implying that we were not very clear. If you want to clarify a previous comment, start with, "What I believe this means is. . . ." or "I hear Gerry saying. . . ." These qualifiers are needed because you don't *really* know what the other person was trying to say.

Questions are often used to clarify, to seek out more information, to eliminate certain possibilities, to make sure the point is complete before moving on. Without clarifying and elaborating, the group may move too quickly, resulting in a superficial analysis or misunderstanding. Another risk of too little elaboration is that you may assume all the data are in place when pieces are missing.

This caution needs to be balanced against the possibility of developing "analysis paralysis," a condition which afflicts many organizations. The need to gather more data, do one more piece of research, find out what every department thinks before acting keeps you from acting decisively. It is a difficult line, but there is a balance between being complete and accurate and being paralyzed.

Summarizing and Evaluating You have seven people in a room at a 90-minute committee meeting. If the time were equally divided, each person will have talked about 13 minutes. A lot of conversation occurred in that time, and different views were expressed. What the group clearly needs is someone to help put these points together into a coherent whole, to reflect accurately what others have said and state simply what has happened thus far. When summarizing, restate different points of view which have been presented, indicate areas of agreement and disagreement, and repeat questions raised which are still unanswered. Summaries should be brief and impartial, that is, they should reflect what the group has done thus far, not just your own thinking. How often have you been at a meeting where the leader said, "Well, then I guess we are all agreed," when it appeared to you and others that no agreement had been reached. This is not a summary but an example of using power to override the group.

Summaries should be done after each major point on the agenda. They serve a number of purposes:

Reminding the group of accomplishments
Focusing attention on the topic
Providing a transition for moving to the next point
Preventing misunderstanding at a later point

If the summary is done well, the group should be
the next item of discussion. It takes a lot of careful liste
rize. If you have been preoccupied with your own cor
not pay much attention to others, you will not be able
summary. When summaries are going to be particularly critical
discussion, you should stay out of the active discussion, ask questions to
clarify, take notes, and from time to time review the group's progress
with your summary.

Consensus Testing Before making a decision, find out where each
person stands on the issues. The purpose of consensus testing is to discover the degree of difference, to define alternatives and priorities, not
to push for agreement. This may take the form of asking if the group is
nearing a decision, discovering areas of agreement and disagreement,
"sending up a trial balloon" to test a possible conclusion, and seeking
common ground.

A good technique for consensus testing is to state the issue and then
go around the table and ask each person to react briefly. Do not allow
discussion to continue during this time until everyone has spoken. If
one or two people have obvious influence on the group, do not start
with them, as they may begin a chain of agreement, when in fact, such
agreement does not exist. Use consensus testing to move out of unnecessary discussion, to get through an impasse, and to check group procedures.

Giving Assignments Many problems will take more than one meeting, necessitating assignments before the group is to meet again. At
staff meetings the manager often has to make assignments for the handling of the workload, for the carrying out of special projects, and for
getting information for a next step. Sometimes it is obvious who needs
to carry out a particular task, so assignment is made easily in these
cases. On other occasions it will be better to ask who wants to do a particular task.

> "Bill, since you have the production records, how about getting the
> monthly data together for the next meeting?"
> "Jane, you have had experience in handling this procedure. Can
> you do an outline?"
> "Ray, your people have made this kind of change before. Why not
> talk to them and report on what problems they encountered?"
> or
> "Who wants to talk to the unit supervisors and find out their per-
> sonnel requirements for next year?"

"Will someone volunteer to go to Financial Controls and get their figures on this?"

"Does one of you have the staff available to research what other companies have done?"

Making assignments can save group time; individuals can do background work rather than everyone struggling with a lack of data and using more time than is necessary.

The makeup of the group and the nature of the task will largely influence how assignments are made. Don't let a meeting close with loose ends that need to be addressed before your next discussion.

Group Maintenance Behaviors

The second set of behaviors needed for effective meetings focuses on how the group is functioning. Group maintenance is often neglected because managers want the group to be completely task-oriented. Helping people to communicate, resolve differences, and feel comfortable with each other is sometimes seen as unnecessary to the work. The work itself and *how* it gets done are inextricably related, thus group maintenance needs as much attention as task maintenance.

Encouraging Participation   At the next meeting you attend, look around the room and notice people's reactions to each other before the meeting begins. Are they talking to each other, smiling, acknowledging a newcomer's presence, and in general getting comfortable? Before and during the meeting, participants react to each other in ways that signal what the environment will be like. Is there a feeling of tension, of opposing sides coming together to do battle, or is this a group which has come together to resolve a problem which matters to everyone?

Many of the ways in which we encourage participation are nonverbal. We set up the room so that people can look at each other instead of at the back of someone else's head, we nod approval or agreement to a comment, or we simply acknowledge another person's presence. There are, of course, more direct ways of encouraging participation, such as asking nonthreatening questions which open up the issues, indicating the need for special knowledge someone else may have, or seeking elaboration on a point.

In addition building on someone else's comments is a way to encourage further contributions. "Anne indicated that her unit had been successful in having clerks handle the service calls. I wonder if the rest of us could try the same approach." This statement lets Anne know that you not only heard, but valued her comment. Minority points of

view need to be supported or the group may overlook vᵣ
butions. This is not to say that tangents should be encou
that people need to feel free to disagree if a problem is to ᵥ
and completely covered.

Gatekeeping   Controlling and directing the flow of communication
is often the leader's primary job at a meeting. There are three primary
ways to be a gatekeeper: encouraging those who haven't participated,
suggesting procedures to regulate the flow of communication, and
managing those who are dominating or disruptive. As there are different responses to each dysfunctional behavior, I deal with such behavior
separately later in this chapter.

Gatekeeping involves being a good listener, both hearing what
people are saying and observing their nonverbal reactions. Watch for
signs that someone is having difficulty breaking into the discussion.
You will see people leaning forward or an expression which indicates
that they have something to say. Some people are more aggressive ver-
bally than others and speak up more quickly or more forcefully.

Another way to encourage participation is to ask a question which
everyone can respond to or to deliberately state that you would like to
hear everyone's view and go around the table until you have heard
from everyone. Ask for specific information from a reticent member if
you are reasonably certain that the person has something to contribute.
Members will resent being called upon if they really have nothing to
say and may add to tangents and waste time. You can suggest procedures such as, "Let's hear from everyone before we move on to the
next item," or, "Each department will have a few minutes to present
its budget before we begin general discussion."

An important factor in gatekeeping is how individuals feel their
comments will be received. When evaluative statements are made before thorough discussion ("That's a terrible idea!"), some will feel discouraged and be unwilling to subject themselves to attack. Your responsibility as a gatekeeper is to keep the channels open, not only to
allow but to encourage full participation.

Reducing Tension   During discussions of matters important to individuals or to the units for which they are responsible, tension is likely.
This is not necessarily harmful, for disagreement is a healthy sign in a
group. But how the disagreements are handled is critical to success of
the group and the accomplishment of the task. Disagreements over issues sometimes become conflict between individuals. Managing differences on issues is covered later in this section. To say, "Let's keep to the

facts and not get personal," is to ignore people's personal investment in a particular point of view or the outcome of a decision. Long-standing hostilities between people cannot necessarily be left outside the conference room door.

Tension may arise simply because it's been a long day, people are tired, or resolution seems impossible. Reducing tension means to mediate personal differences between members. You can do this by helping them to explore differences, moving to another topic, inviting others to participate, or using humor. Be careful not to be sarcastic or put a group member down. The message is not lost on others who may become reluctant to participate and unwilling to risk the sarcasm of the leader or another member.

Clarifying Communication   Throughout this book communication has been described as a process of trying to understand another's meaning. Realizing that experience gives rise to different meanings for the same words will help you to see the need for clarifying communication. A great deal of time is consumed in meetings by people responding to their own meaning and not to what actually was said. If people seem to be talking past each other or making assumptions which have not been checked out, you should try to clarify the communication. Paraphrasing is an excellent technique which can be used on these occasions: "What I heard Gary saying is . . ." or, "Before we continue I want to check back with Al to see if we understood his point." This simple way of checking out meaning enables the group to refocus their attention on the original comment and try to achieve a common degree of understanding. If you don't understand what someone has said, ask for an example, summarize the key points, or simply say, "I don't understand what you mean." Be careful not to interpret and tell what *you* think the person was really trying to say. Only reflect what was actually said. If one or more members are having difficulty understanding each other, ask them to paraphrase before the discussion continues.

Nearly everyone has had the experience of going to a meeting, then reading the minutes or talking to someone else who attended and wondering if they were at the same meeting. If seven people are in the room, seven sets of meaning will develop. You cannot achieve complete understanding, only work to minimize misunderstanding so that your goals are met.

Managing Differences   One of the reasons meetings are called is that people have different sets of information and different points of view. Some conflict, then, is inevitable. If you are uncomfortable with people disagreeing, and try to minimize differences before they are fully explored, the quality of the decision will be reduced.

The first thing to do with a disagreement is to make the differences explicit.[5] Too often managers will gloss over differences in an effort to achieve harmony. Ask how this person's view differs from that of others. Use questions to clarify and discover if there is a real difference. Paraphrase to accurately reflect what has been stated. Check out assumptions which may not have been tested.

Once the various positions are clearly stated, work toward resolving the differences. To keep the discussion on the issues and not on people, acknowledge the validity of the position for that person; seek to understand it before you counter with your own arguments. Often differences are muddled because so many points are being dealt with at one time. Stick to one point at a time, outline the key issues, use summaries as you move along, and try consensus testing to discover the degree of difference.

Differences can be based on distortions of information, biases in judgment, failure to listen, and individual, rather than group, goals. Differences also legitimately arise when people have accurate information and judgment, have listened, and are aware of group goals. One of the keys to an effective organization is the ability to balance some built-in conflicts. Marketing and manufacturing have differences which result from their separate roles in the organization. The differences should not be submerged or ignored, but rather brought into the open so problems can be resolved.

Managing differences requires flexible behavior, the ability to change your mind when a strong case has been made, to acknowledge the difficulties experienced by someone else, and to consider options rather than one course of action. Task accomplishment can be greatly enhanced by someone who is skillful in managing differences.

SELF-ORIENTED BEHAVIORS

If you have attended more than one meeting in your career, you have probably encountered people whose behavior is disruptive and dysfunctional. They are oriented toward the self rather than toward the needs of the group. All of us, at one time or another, act in a self-oriented manner. When you encounter behavior disruptive to others, you need to know how to respond to the self-oriented individual.

---

[5] These concepts are based on material supplied by Billie Alban.

You can find a number of descriptions of self-oriented behaviors in various books on leadership and conferences. The ones discussed here are most common to groups in organizations. You can add to the list.

Blocking
Seeking recognition
Dominating
Using status
Irrelevant response
Disapproving
Working a hidden agenda

Blocking   Blocking means someone is disagreeing long after most have come to agreement, bringing back an issue clearly rejected by the group, opposing something without clear reasons or in contradiction to the available data. Do not confuse the need for the group to disagree, as discussed earlier, with blocking.

When confronted by this behavior, try to move the discussion to the next point. You can request that the objection be considered privately or at a later time, summarize, and then move to a new issue, limiting the amount of time to be given to further discussion. Honestly try to find merit in one of the points to help the blocking person feel at ease and accepted by the group.

Seeking Recognition   As with other activities in organizations, meetings can be used to advance personal status. Some members may want to get a favorite view across for their own credit, others may need to gain recognition by long or technical explanations. The signals of seeking recognition are excessively calling attention to oneself by unusual behavior such as coming in late and bursting into the discussion, boasting, and reporting on personal achievements. A person who is seeking recognition will have a hard time giving the floor to others and may have difficulty seeing the validity of others' comments.

Respond to someone who is seeking recognition at the expense of the group by acknowledging the person's contributions (where you can do so honestly), emphasize the group's goals, try to see how the comments fit into the discussion. If all else fails, change to a different topic on the agenda. You may find that a talk between meetings is needed to reassure the recognition seeker. You need to be sensitive to what may be anxiety on this individual's part, without sacrificing the legitimate recognition of the other members.

Dominating   Who of us has not dominated at one meeting or another? Perhaps the topic made you loquacious, or your expertise was needed for most of the points on the agenda. There are times when it is appropriate for an individual to take up a significant amount of the group's time. A dominating person who is self-oriented, however, tries to manipulate the group, interrupts others, frequently talks when others are speaking, and is unaware when others want to speak.

The odds of one person being able to dominate are lessened if the group is composed of individuals who will voice their opinions readily. Dominating, after all, means that those who do not dominate go along and are silent for a time. You may wish to give the dominating person some feedback after the meeting and discuss ways that the disruptor can contribute without taking over the group. During the meeting, be prepared to involve others, to ask questions that will generate another point of view, or deliberately start with someone else when introducing a new topic. If the comments have gone on too long, be prepared to break in when the person takes a breath and to move to another issue or a different person. Respond positively to some part of what was said, but don't, at the same time, encourage a new round of dominating behavior.

Using Status   Solving problems is best done where status comes from experience, knowledge, and expertise, not from position in the hierarchy. Although most would agree with that statement, the reality often is that the person who carries the title of director, vice president, executive vice president, or regional manager has more influence than others at the meeting. This presents special problems to the leader and the other participants. The situation is especially difficult if the person who called the meeting is not the one with the most status in the group. Fortunately, some people are able to handle their roles and do not try and exert special influence on the group. Others, either directly or by implication, may use their positions to sway the group, to evaluate the comments of participants, or even to insist on a particular course of action. Handling someone like this at a meeting calls for great tact and skill.

If you know someone who is likely to use status to the detriment of the group, use the guidelines given under "planning schedules" earlier in the chapter to avoid inviting that person to the meeting. If you cannot avoid the situation, plan techniques in advance to try and control the behavior. Invite others who are strong enough to express views independently, prepare a clear and full agenda, be ready to use information to make the best possible case, use consensus testing, and leave this person until last to reduce the possibility of influence.

Irrelevant Response   Keeping a meeting on track can be a difficult task, especially when the group is large or represents multiple points of view. Determining just what is relevant is not always easy. Most often irrelevant responses come from people who have not been listening or who are so concerned about their own point of view that they do not acknowledge what others have said. Introducing a new topic without warning, or bringing up information which has little bearing on the point are both irrelevant responses. In any meeting, a few comments will be less relevant than others. The plant manager thinks he is illustrating a point on service by relating the way he handled a machine problem to the purchase of new equipment for the home office, but others miss the connection. Here, however, we are concerned about the person who consistently sidetracks the discussion and takes time for matters that need not be dealt with at the meeting.

You have to make a judgment as to how this person will react to questioning before deciding how to handle the situation. You can ask in an objective way how the point related to the discussion, but do not attack. If you say, "That doesn't have any bearing that I can see; explain it," in a threatening tone of voice, the person may further elaborate only to defend the position. You may acknowledge the comment briefly and then move on to a summary, ask for others' reactions to guide the discussion in a new direction. If you are using an agenda, refer to it and check with the group as to whether or not they want to spend time on this particular topic. Offer to discuss the point with the person outside the meeting, or call the group's attention to the time limits for this meeting.

Aggressing   When members are behaving aggressively, they frequently disapprove of the values and feelings of others. Notice this does not say that they disagree with ideas or information. Aggressing is a much more personalized behavior. Another way to be aggressive is to deflate the status or position of others: "People in research never do know what goes on." Or an individual may take credit for other members' contributions.

The person who behaves aggressively at meetings may need reassurance as to the value of his or her contributions; give recognition without undue flattery. Be sure to give credit to each person for his or her ideas. If disapproval is expressed, try and find out the basis for that disapproval; if appropriate, discuss further.

Hidden Agenda An individual's behavior at a meeting may appear confusing because of personal goals which are not clear to others. Some members may be aware that the individual has a private goal but there is tacit agreement to pretend they do not know. For example, organizations have topics which are "taboo," things that everyone knows about but no one discusses.[6] The hidden agenda may be a taboo topic or could stem from personal goals. People with hidden agendas can consume a lot of time and undermine the group.

At a meeting to select a manager for a new field office, the vice president of the eastern region may reject all the candidates without clearly stating the reasons. This vice president may have a particular candidate in mind who will be suggested after the group has apparently rejected everyone else. This spirit of covert competition can be most destructive because it cannot be dealt with openly.

When planning a meeting, you may realize the potential of some hidden agendas. One possibility is simply to ask each person for personal (or functional unit) goals, openly recognizing that such goals exist. This could get some of the agendas into the open where you can at least deal with them. You may need to spend time with individuals on a one-to-one basis outside the meeting to find out more about their needs and how the group is seen. Helping a person to understand and be committed to the group goals can be a powerful way to reduce the impact of hidden agendas. When membership in the group becomes important, private goals may recede.

LEADERSHIP AND MEETINGS

People have widely varying beliefs and feelings about leadership and what is the most effective way to behave as the leader in a group. Although there are many approaches to this topic, a view which has been most useful is to define the leader as a person seen by the group members as having influence and helping to fulfill their needs.

This definition implies a functional approach to leadership which emphasizes what the leader *does*. In the functional view, leadership is shared; any and all members of the group may perform specific leadership acts or functions, such as stating a goal, summarizing, or encouraging others to speak. These functions must be supplied by someone if the group is to reach its objectives.

---

[6] Fritz Steele, *The Open Organization: The Impact of Secrecy and Disclosure on People and Organizations* (Reading, Mass.: Addison–Wesley, 1975), ch. 12.

The functional approach to leadership requires a new set of skills, including the ability to diagnose the situation and determine the appropriate style of leadership. This does not imply that the leader must be a chameleon and change colors to blend into the environment, only that a leader must be aware of options and exercise them.

Problems facing organizations and organizational problem solvers are so varied and complex that no one style of leadership can suit all situations. The answer to, "Who is an effective leader?" is, "It all depends" on the person, the other group members and the situation.[7] The leader is the person who can help the group function as well as exert influence over other members. The leader's source of influence may come from the position in the organization as well as how he or she behaves with group members. For purposes of this discussion leaders are not people who can get others to do what they desire, but those who can help the group to achieve results. Achieving results includes not only task accomplishment, but individual satisfaction with participation and pride in the accomplishments of the group.

POSTMEETING ACTIVITIES

Like many managers today, you may have meetings at 9:00 a.m. at 10:30, at 12:15 for luncheon, and possibly at 2:30 or 3:00. While this is not a schedule you would want every day, it is hardly unusual in its number of meetings. As you literally run from one meeting to another, you are lucky if you have the right material along and show up in the right room. On other days perhaps only one or two meetings are scheduled. It's rare for managers to have days without meetings. No matter what the constraints of time, it is important to develop some way of doing follow-up on meetings you attend. Each manager will have personal devices such as a tickler file, a pocket calendar, or a list for each day. Doing follow-up is an important factor in contributing to the success of the next meeting. Instead of just thinking what you have to do or remembering what assignment you were given, try to review the whole meeting more systematically.

Review the Goal

Did you achieve the goals of the meeting? If not, why not? What could have been done differently? What can you do about task or group

[7] Robert Tannenbaum and Warren Schmidt, "How To Choose a Leadership Pattern," *Harvard Business Review*, May–June 1973, p. 182.

maintenance behaviors which were missing from the meeting? Can you do something to contribute to achieving the goal of the next meeting? Is there someone to talk to in the meantime?

Identify Personal Responsibilities

What is expected of you now? Are you to get some information, interview people for opinions, check a policy, develop a budget, prepare a report, or inform others of what happened at the meeting? Be sure you make a record of your obligation and indicate a deadline. Often we forget about our commitments until just before the next meeting and then start scrambling around to get them accomplished. Perhaps you can delegate some part of your assignment. In any case make plans to be prepared for the next session.

Evaluate Your Own Participation

Overall were you as effective as you might have been? If not, why not? What factors were there in the situation that interfered with your effectiveness? Which kinds of task maintenance contributions did you make? If you find that you contributed information but did not ask questions, plan to try that behavior in the next meeting. Which group maintenance behaviors were missing? For example, did people get confused because of a lengthy discussion without a summary? Even if you were not the leader; it should be possible to provide some of these needed behaviors for the group. If the discussion got off on a tangent, did you wait for the leader to bring it back? Might you have done something to refocus the group yourself? Practice saying what you might have said in the circumstances. Vowing to eliminate tangents will not help unless you are prepared the next time to say, "I think that's an individual problem and we need to get back to the issue."

If You Called the Meeting, Assess Your Leadership Effectiveness   Based on your analysis of the group members, the nature of the task, and your own leadership behavior, how effective were you in working with the group? Did they respond to your direction and listen to your summaries? How active were members in participating? What was their reaction to you and to each other? Did you accomplish what you needed to in the time available? What do you need to do differently at the next meeting?

Clarify the goals.
Provide more or less structure. ⟩

Work to include the more reticent members.

Control those who are being dysfunctional.

Find out more about what members want to get out of this project.

Use each meeting you attend to monitor your leadership behavior in relation to achieving goals. Are you sacrificing the task for the sake of good relationships or avoiding conflict to preserve harmony? By paying attention to what you did do and what you could do, the quality of leadership can be improved.

Check the Use of Time

How effectively was the time used? Did you get through the agenda or only finish the first two items? It may be that you didn't get further if the agenda was too ambitious or if the group fround more discussion was needed on a particular point, but if you feel the time was not used well, focus on where the group could have been more efficient. Was too much time devoted to one issue or to one person? Were too many tangents allowed? Did the group flounder because of lack of information and pursue an issue which should have been delayed until more data were available? Were self-oriented behaviors blocking the meeting? If so, how could they be dealt with the next time? What preparation would help people make better use of the time at the next meeting?

Identify the Goal of the Next Meeting

Given what was accomplished, what does the group have to do the next time? Is a meeting necessary to achieve the goal, or would the time be better spent on individual work before getting together again? If there is no reason to meet, don't even if the time is scheduled. Are members clear about the goal of the next meeting? A lot of time can be lost redoing the work of earlier meetings. A brief recap can help, but try not to go over ground already covered unless there is new information or another significant reason to do so.

Evaluate the General Health of the Group

A group which is healthy possesses many of the characteristics of a mature individual. It is flexible, adaptable, has clear communication with others and a capacity to process and respond to information from the environment. Getting work done at meetings relies on a number of individuals being able to act collectively as a mature entity. Given the competing interests and various conflicts inherent in every organization, it is not possible to have a "mature" group all the time. Overall you should be looking for a group to meet the following criteria:[8]

1. Is the group able to get information that it needs and to process it?
2. Does the group have the capacity to respond to and deal realistically with the environment?
3. Is there a basic agreement within the group about goals and values?
4. Does the group make optimum use of the resources available within the group?
5. Does the group have the capacity for self-knowledge? Are members aware of the impact of their behavior on each other? Do they understand why they are doing what they are doing?
6. Does the group have the capacity to learn from its experience? Is new information assimilated and responded to?
7. Are the group's internal processes—communication, decision making, distribution of authority—integrated into the task accomplishment?

Examining these dimensions can help the group study itself and see weak spots in its operation. Then, like any healthy organism, the group can operate in a self-correcting way, rather than continuing processes which are detrimental to members and the task.

SUMMARY

The nature of modern organizations requires managers to spend nearly half their time at meetings. This is especially true in the areas of policy, where objectives are determined, long-range planning occurs, personnel policy is established, and all forms of regulative communication take place. The time expended at meetings and the impact of decisions requires managers to be skillful in conducting and participating in meetings.

Knowledge of three categories of meeting behavior—task, maintenance, and self-oriented—can help to get work done at meetings. You have to pay attention to both the task and the maintenance functioning of the group. Self-oriented behaviors can be dysfunctional and need to be minimized.

---

[8] Edgar Schein, *Process Consultation: Its Role in Organization Development* (Reading, Mass.: Addison–Wesley, 1968).

The most effective leader and group members are those who have a repertoire of behavior. These are people who can adjust to differences in the task and makeup of the group. *An important rule of thumb is never to do for the group what it can do for itself.* If members occasionally provide summaries or are doing well asking pertinent questions, then, let it go. You may notice that no one is gatekeeping or initiating procedures, and this is what would be best for you to do.

At many meetings contributing information will be your most common behavior. If you are the leader, however, you should leave the bulk of the discussion to the other participants. By being actively involved in the guts of the discussion, your ability to listen to the group and to do the maintenance functions will be limited. In order to assess what members need to accomplish the task, you need to be free to listen. Planning and a carefully thought out agenda will help free you.

The balance between task and relationships among members is critical; one is seldom (in an organizational setting) more important than another. If you pay exclusive attention to relationships, people may like each other but not necessarily accomplish very much. Eventually the lack of task accomplishment will become frustrating, and people will withdraw from the group. [A group which is very task oriented and pays little attention to relationships can be very productive in some circumstances. But in any prolonged work situation the difficulties in relationships—not feeling free to speak, people dominating, disagreements which don't surface—will affect productivity and the capacity of the group to implement solutions.] The balance of task and group maintenance behaviors may shift, and you need to be equipped to analyze the situation to determine which behavior will be most useful to the group.

After the meeting is over, analyze your objectives and your behavior. What might you have done, regardless of who was the leader, to make the group more effective? What are your responsibilities for the next meeting? In what ways has your behavior changed in the last few weeks? If you are contributing more effectively, give yourself some positive feedback! Use the case studies which follow to plan a meeting. Then fill out the self-assessment forms in preparation for your personal communication plan.

CASE STUDIES

CASE 1

Setting: Industrial Manufacturing
Your Position: Vice President, Plastics Division

Your corporation manufactures plastics and other synthetic materials used largely by the automotive industry. You have five plants located in Michigan (2), Ohio (2), and Indiana (1). Employees in these locations include 100 middle and senior managers, 250 supervisors, and nearly 5,000 hourly workers.

The Environmental Protection Agency has asked your division to do away with a number of violations. Three plants can be modified (at some expense) to comply with EPA guidelines. The Detroit plant and the Akron plant, however, may have to be closed. They are both old and inefficient and were scheduled to be phased out over the next five years. No one was aware of these plans including the plant managers.

The President recently approved a new facility, and you have investigated three sites for it. None presumes any particular problems or advantages, although the Flint location is closer to your primary market.

A decision on which site to choose must be made soon as the option on the Ohio site will expire soon. The third site is in a new industrial park in Illinois. Because of the costs of housing in the new locations, and commuting problems in Michigan, the plant managers are likely to have strong opinions about the new location. Also, during the phase-out period, employees who are scheduled to be laid off are likely to be dissatisfied.

You have called a meeting of plant managers at corporate headquarters in Detroit.

Questions:

What is the goal of the meeting?
What information should the plant managers receive in advance?
What information should they be asked to bring on their plant?
Who else should be invited?
What will be the major blocks in making a decision?
Which task/maintenance behaviors will be most important?
Assume that some of the managers will engage in self-oriented behavior. What coping responses are available to you?
Outline an agenda.
Write a memo announcing the meeting.

CASE 2

Setting: Long-Term Health Care Facilities
Your Position: Director of Convalescent Care

MLTCA (Municipal Long-Term Convalescent Agency) operates eleven convalescent centers. Six of the facilities were acquired by purchase of private nursing homes. The others were hospitals which have been converted for long-term care.

As Director of Convalescent Care, you report directly to a County Commissioner, who has requested that you develop a plan for two intensive care centers. These two new facilities will draw patients from the existing centers, thus enabling better care for special illnesses and relieving the convalescent centers from the expense of maintaining highly specialized equipment.

You need to define a selection procedure to determine which patients are most in need of these special care facilities. Your center directors will have responsibility for applying these criteria. Some of the directors have definite ideas about maintaining a mix of patients. Many of them are reluctant to transfer patients because they feel their center can give better care than any other institution. In addition changes in staffing will be necessitated to provide needed medical, nursing, and social services.

Questions

Should you have a meeting to make this decision?
If your answer is yes, see questions in section B.
If your answer is no, see questions in Section A.

Section A

1. What information do you need to make the decision?
2. How will you get it?
3. What difficulties are you hoping to avoid by not holding a meeting?
4. What plans will you make to implement your decision?

Section B

1. What is the goal of the meeting?
2. What information do participants need in advance?
3. Given the potential for conflict, what behaviors will you need to help the group to manage differences?
4. What are the obstacles to the group making a decision in any reasonable period of time?
5. Outline a tentative agenda.

PREMEETING ACTIVITIES FOR ONE WHO CALLS THE MEETING

1. Goal for this meeting is:

2. People who should attend the meeting:

   People who need to attend who may not be helpful:

3. Information which I need and/or should get to participants:

4. Order of steps to achieve goal:

5. Working agenda with approximate time for each item:

6. Appropriate leadership style and needed behaviors:

PREMEETING ACTIVITIES FOR ONE WHO ATTENDS THE MEETING

1. Goal of the meeting is:

2. Reason for being asked:

3. Information I need:

4. My purpose is:

5. Task behaviors which will be most needed:

6. Maintenance behaviors which will be most needed:

SELF-ASSESSMENT OF MEETING SKILLS

Use the scale on the right to help assess your skill in carrying out each task or behavior for improving meetings. Your evaluation should be based on: (1) ability to perform the task or behavior, (2) knowing when each is appropriate or needed at a meeting, (3) willingness to actually engage in the behavior. The scale ranges from 1 (low) to 5 (high). After you have assessed each item listed, review your behavior and place a ✔ in the column to the far right indicating if you are satisfied or dissatisfied with your skill level.

Task Behaviors	1	2	3	4	5	Satisfied	Dissatisfied
1. *Initiating* goals and procedures to help a group organize their task.						___	___
2. *Seeking information*, getting others' opinions, information.						___	___
3. *Giving information*, providing own views of topic.						___	___
4. *Clarifying* terms which are ambiguous, *elaborating* on ideas.						___	___
5. *Summarizing* different points of view.						___	___
6. Checking for *consensuses*; determining areas of agreement or disagreement.						___	___
7. *Giving assignments* or directions for the next meeting.						___	___

	Dissatisfied 1	2	3	4	5 Satisfied

Maintenance Behaviors

1. *Encouraging* others by indicating acceptance.
2. *Harmonizing* by reducing tension; exploring personal differences between others.
3. *Managing differences* by exploring issues between self and others.
4. *Gatekeeping* to help everyone to participate, keeping the channels of communication open.
5. *Clarifying communication* by reflecting back what was said, asking others to restate what they heard before continuing.

Premeeting Planning

1. Discover goal of meeting.
2. Identify reasons for being asked.
3. Identify necessary info and act.
4. Identify own purpose for attending meeting.
5. If I call the meeting, go through necessary planning steps.

Postmeeting Planning

	1	2	3	4	5	Satisfied	Dissatisfied
1. Review goal achievement.							
2. Identify personal responsibilities.							
3. Evaluate my participation.							
4. Assess the use of time.							
5. Determine goal of next meeting.							

Problem Solving

	1	2	3	4	5	Satisfied	Dissatisfied
1. Able to follow problem solving sequence to determine my contributions.							
2. Able to use problem solving sequence to set appropriate agenda when I call a meeting.							
3. Able to use problem solving sequence to help a group manage their time and information.							

PROBLEM SOLVING OUTLINE

1. Problem definition
   a. What background and/or prior decisions might help in understanding the problem?
   b. What specific aspects will be *included* in the problem?
      (1) Are any *excluded* aspects vital to understanding the problem?
      (2) What time period is appropriate when considering the problem? (For example, how far in the past and in the future should be considered?)
   c. Is there understanding of and agreement on the key terms in the problem statement?
   d. Does everyone agree on the nature of the problem?

If any needed information is missing, allow enough time before scheduling the next meeting for it to be gathered, distributed, and read.

2. Problem analysis
   a. Causes
      (1) What are the causes of the problem?
      (2) Are there other causes which are not readily apparent?
      (3) Are the causes which have been identified sufficient to cause the problem?
         (a) Is the problem the product of a single cause or several?
         (b) Can a direct connection between cause(s) and problem be established? In other words, is the relationship other than coincidence?
         (c) Which cause(s) is having the most impact on the problem? (Check out what happens if each cause is eliminated.)
      (4) What is the probability of your being able to influence each of these causes?
   b. Consequences
      (1) What are the consequences of the problem?
      (2) Who or what is being affected by the problem?
      (3) What specifically are the effects?
      (4) What is the magnitude of each effect (quantitative and qualitative)?
      (5) What are the short-term and long-term consequences? (Refer back to part 1, b, 2.)

(6) As a result of all previous discussion, which effects seem to be the most detrimental?

If the consequences are not significant and/or the group cannot influence the causes, consider alternative actions. (For example, disband the group and report to senior management.)

3. Criteria for acceptable solution
   a. What causes and/or consequences must a solution reduce or eliminate in order to be acceptable?
   b. What criteria must an acceptable solution meet? Is it feasible from the points of view of finance law, corporate policy, manpower, time?
   c. What kinds of new and significant problems must be avoided in devising a solution?

4. Available solutions
   a. What are the possible solutions to this problem?
   b. Who else has had a simlilar problem, what have they done, and with what results?
   c. What would be the ideal solution from the point of view of all parties involved in the problem?

5. Selection of best solution
   a. Of the solutions offered, which seems best when evaluated using the criteria generated in step 3?
   b. Is there a way of combining any of the suggestions in order to arrive at the best solution?
   c. Can everyone agree on a statement of the solution?
   d. What are the implications of your solution? Can you gain appropriate commitment? What difficulties will have to be overcome to make the solution work?

6. Plan for implementation
   a. What has to be done by whom and by when?
   b. What resources are needed?
   c. Who needs to know about the decision and how will it be communicated?
   d. How will the effectiveness of the solution be evaluated?

CHAPTER 4
EXPLAINING POLICIES
AND PROCEDURES

Imagine that someone enters 'your organization who has no prior knowledge of its products or services. How would you explain how the organization works, the policies which govern employment, the workflow, and the technical procedures?

ROLE OF EXPLANATIONS IN TASK COMMUNICATION

How does a press punch machine work?

What does a claims analyst do to determine payment under a health care plan?

How does raw fiber get transformed into textiles?

What are the benefits for an employee who takes early retirement?

What are the input procedures for the on-line computer system?

What does a bank teller do if confronted by a robbery?

How do you close down a machine when materials are faulty?

What are the guidelines governing conflict of interest for bank officers?

What cutbacks will be made in your agency due to the loss of federal funding?

Each of these is a question describing a situation which calls for a good explanation. Explaining policies and procedures is a continuous communication job for the manager and makes up the bulk of task communication in an organization.

TABLE 4.1 Log for Giving Explanations

Topic	Time	Persons	Policy	Procedure	Work-related
1.					
2.					
3.					
4.					
5.					

TABLE 4.2 Example of Log for Director of Hospital Emergency Room

Topic	Time	Persons	Policy	Procedure	Work-related
1. New form for admitting patients	20	Admissions clerk		X	
2. Operation of lab equipment	30	New lab technician			X
3. Why waiting time is so long	5	Parent of injured child			X
4. Vacation policy	7	Registered nurse	X		
5. What lab test to perform	4	Emergency room nurse		X	X

To determine just how much explaining you do in a day, use the log in Table 4.1 to track the topic, the audience, the amount of time, and the type of explanation. The log in Table 4.2 for a supervisor in a hospital emergency room covers only the first few hours of duty. Depending, of course, on the nature of your job and the degree of technology in the work, explanations can consume a significant amount of time.

One of your responsibilities, then, no matter what your level in the organization, is to be a link between the needs of the organization and those of the employees. At times, these needs may conflict; they are often balanced through administration of policies and procedures. The need for policy and procedures is dictated by the size and complexity of modern organizations: The AT&T system numbers nearly 1 million people in its organization; General Motors has over 800,000; and IBM, more than 300,000. With so many people working for the same company, policies are needed to assure fairness and consistency as well as to inform people of the guidelines for behavior under differing circumstances. Small organizations often find policies and procedures are needed as well.

Procedures are required to see to it that work is done consistently, in conformance to routines, and meeting legal or organizational requirements. Small organizations may operate less formally, yet will need to explain conditions of employment and how the work is to be done.

Whatever the size of your organization, employees need to know its policies and procedures. The task of communicating this information is a formidable one. Employees generally see their immediate boss as the most important source of information in the organization.[1] As that source for a number of employees, your skills in explaining policy, procedures, and work-related matters are important to your overall effectiveness.

ROLE OF POLICY AND PROCEDURES

A policy should define philosophy, provide direction, and establish guidelines for behavior. Procedures, on the other hand, are more exacting and detailed, instructions on how to carry out the policy. The poli-

---

[1] Gerald M. Goldhaber, Michael P. Yates, D. Thomas Porter, and Richard Lesniak, "State of the Art, Organizational Communication: 1978, *"Human Communication Research,* Volume 5, no. 1 Fall, 1978. p. 82.

cy may state, "It is our policy to pay equally for equal work." The procedures will probably have complicated instructions for evaluating jobs, credentials, and length of service. The procedures help you implement the policy and attempt to assure fair and consistent treatment. But the policy guides and overrules. Policies have to be interpreted and should allow some alternatives for the particular situation.

When a policy manual tries to cover every possible exception, it ends up as a long set of rules which require a technical expert. In some areas of policy, such as compensation and benefits, expertise and special communication skills are required. In general, your policy manual should express how the organization intends to treat people. Procedures help consistency of interpretation and prevent the capriciousness that has been known to be part of some managers' behavior.

Most organizations have two primary sets of information for employees: personnel policies and procedures which affect the employee as an individual and those matters which are task related. Task-related information has to do with how a job is to be performed, where the work must go, by when, and how it's formed. As a member of the organization, employees should know the organization's views of how they are going to be treated. A checklist of policies and procedures that an organization should have is included at the end of the chapter.

At times you may be in the unenviable position of explaining a policy with which you don't agree. This poses a dilemma to managers. Do you tell employees that you support the new salary policy, or that, in fact, you don't agree with it? Or are you copping out when you say, "I wouldn't have done it this way, but that's how Personnel wants it." Somewhere between those two extremes is the line for the manager who is communicating with integrity. In general don't blame others—top management or personnel—but describe the policy as fully as you can and trust the employee to make a reasonable judgment. Don't forget that your credibility is your most important resource in communication. It can overcome many a technically flawed explanation.

GUIDELINES FOR GIVING EXPLANATIONS

All of us have experienced a communication breakdown after giving what seemed like a good explanation. We wonder why the other person didn't understand what we said. Explanations are a two-way, interactive process which is the result of what you say, how you say it, and what the other person perceives. You must accept some responsibility for providing as clear an explanation as possible.

Giving clear explanations is simply another example of effective communication. The principles of communication discussed in other chapters need to be remembered—for example, understanding that individuals respond out of personal experience, not necessarily only to the words you use. This principle of communication—meaning lies in the person and not in the words—holds true when you are giving explanations as well as other communication activities. Paralanguage and nonverbal language also will affect the quality of an explanation.

Explanations are given in a variety of circumstances as indicated by your log. Assigning work is one of the most frequent types of explanation a manager gives. Assignments are given for committee work, for reorganization, for new projects, for meeting production goals, for operating equipment, and other aspects of maintaining the work unit. On-the-job training is another common situation which calls for clear explanations.

Clear explanations are also necessary when things change, as they so often do in any organization. It may be a new policy, a procedure required by the government, or by your own quality control department. Whatever the circumstances, the explanation must be complete, accurate, and clear enough for others to follow.

Most managers intend to give clear explanations and are often puzzled when confusion results. Explanations can fail for a number of reasons: inappropriate language; too much or too little information; inconsistency in symbolic, nonverbal, or paralanguage; or the employee's expectations may differ vastly from reality. You can control some (although not all) of these difficulties by following seven key points in giving explanations:

1. Identify a purpose for your topic.
2. Select the appropriate media.
3. Limit the number of ideas.
4. Use language with a common frame of reference.
5. Include transitions and summaries.
6. Don't overqualify the information.
7. Allow for feedback.

Identify a Purpose for Your Topic

In giving a good explanation, no matter how short or how long it may be, it is important initially to identify two items: (1) the topic and (2) your purpose. Most often managers will identify the topic, but fail to include the purpose.

You want to tell your unit about the needed increase in production, but it may not be clear why this particular item is being explained. The why gives the listener a context; it helps to sort out which information is relevant and which is not. For the listener the why is a motivator, a matter of interest, and a frame of reference. Any given topic can have many different purposes. Let's look at an example: The budget process is being changed to charge each area for all expenses on an "as used" basis. Prior to this, you were charged a pro rata amount for all services, such as building space, duplicating, and training. There can be a variety of purposes for the explanation, such as sharing information, changing behavior or problem solving.

Management Information   The first purpose could be for information only. The new report is of general interest to managers and to those who handle the budget process, but it may have no particular impact on their work. A great deal of information is given or explained to help people understand what is going on in an organization without apparent or direct impact on their work, behavior, or productivity. It does, however, affect their perception of themselves as members of the organization. Knowing what is going on before it happens is one of the ways you can aid this perception. Rather than seeing new expense figures in a report, managers are given advance warning by a small and brief explanation marked, "For information only."

Change in Behavior   Another reason for giving explanations is that a change in behavior is expected. A change in the method of reporting costs may require people to alter their work process, to whom they send data, or the amount of work that they perform. In each of these cases the impact is a direct one and action is required. The explanation has to stimulate the person as well as give a clear course of action which will fulfill the required goals.

In this example budget administrators and people who request services and supplies will need to change their behavior. The budget administrator will have to incorporate into budget preparation costs projected by staff areas. A supervisor will need to know how much material is copied in the duplicating department and may study ways to reduce costs.

Problem Solving   Of course, a topic may be explained because the recipient needs to participate in the discussion of issues and contribute solutions. This particular purpose calls for a completely different frame of reference for the listener. Rather than just storing information, the person is asked to analyze the problem and to contribute to the solution.

If you were the manager of data processing in this case, a number of people would need to study current operations and develop computer programs for charges to be made to other units. One of the reasons that explanations might go awry is that you do not communicate a clear purpose. Consequently your listener has increased opportunity to misinterpret your message.

This discussion is not meant to limit the amount of information a manager provides. Rather it is meant to encourage clear, purposeful communication. We have such an abundance of information today that it is impossible for everyone to remember what is most important. A clear, well-stated purpose is the first step in giving a clear explanation.

Select the Appropriate Media

The printed word is held sacred in many organizations. We often think that if an item is in print, it has to be true and is of more value. Yet print is used so much that most people in organizations are inundated with material. Employees generally prefer oral, face-to-face communication to print or other impersonal media. Selection of media should be made after analyzing the purpose of the intended message and the size and location of the audience. The preference of the individuals in the organization is an additional consideration in media selection. Employees who have grown up with television are used to visual, brief, and timely presentations of information.

Research has shown that group meetings are typically regarded as a highly effective medium of downward communication and that the spoken word is better than the written word for trying to effect attitude change. The role of print is usually to reinforce existing views and to transform uncertainty into a definite opinion. Print is, of course, also helpful for information which is constant and is used repeatedly. The choice of media is seldom an either–or proposition since a combination of oral and written media is more effective than either oral or written presentations by themselves.[2]

Functions of Print   Print, when used appropriately, offers several advantages to the manager:

---

[2] W. Charles Redding, *Communication Within the Organization* (New York: Industrial Communication Council, 1972), pp. 461–477.

Permanence
Retrievability
Repetition
Documentation
Ability to reach large audiences simultaneously

Each of these advantages has its place in communication. Unfortunately most of us never remember to ask whether or not this particular information has to be in print. It has, in most organizations, become a reflex action to pick up the pen or to dictate a memo.

Print also has benefits for the person giving the explanation. It allows us to rethink our ideas, to search for exactly the right word, and to reorganize the order of the material. And print provides visual clues. When an explanation is given in writing, such things as underlining, paragraphing, and italics can be used to aid the reader in interpretation.

Functions of Oral Communication   Oral communication, whether in person or over the phone, relies on the voice for interpretive clues. Your voice conveys the visual impact of paragraphs, punctuation, or underlining. Your tone of voice, timing, and emphasis on certain words all communicate a great deal to your audience. At the same time, this richness of communication in your voice is open for misinterpretation. What is really impatience or fatigue on your part may be read as anger by someone else. The message, then, is totally changed.

The advantages of oral communication are:

Immediacy
Opportunity for feedback
Personal and informal
Encompasses two media, sound and nonverbal cues

When you select oral communication for your explanation, you can very quickly get a response from others by asking questions or by looking at them. Another element of immediacy has to do with feedback. Feedback is the ability to get a response and to alter or adjust your behavior in such a way as to make the communication more meaningful. In most oral communication situations, it is possible to get a response from the other person to adjust your message for increased clarity and understanding.

A third advantage of oral communication is that it is more personal and informal. Employees like to hear "the word" from a direct source; often their department head is only a name to them. If an explanation is of critical importance to your organization—such as a change in reporting relationships—seeing and hearing the manager has an impact which cannot be achieved in print.

Last, in oral communication more media are available to people to grasp the meaning of the explanation. Earlier it was pointed out that employees prefer face-to-face communication. Because it provides more clues for interpretation and an opportunity for feedback, oral communication provides the opportunity to check out the accuracy of what a particular word or idea may have meant.

In large organizations you often need to reach audiences in the thousands. One of the limits of oral communication is that you can reach relatively few people at a given time. If you want to tell a large number of people the same information, you may have to have a series of meetings in order to reach all of them, or you may choose print as the best medium for the situation.

Another limitation is that it is difficult to follow technical language or detailed figures in oral communication. That kind of information is best understood using two channels. If you are going to present technical data, you might do it orally in a meeting. At the same time, you would want to use slides or other visuals to increase the audience's retention.

You can select the appropriate media or combination by examining the contrast below:

Written Information	Oral Information
Can be filed for recall.	May be forgotten through memory lapse.
Is an exact record of events.	Provides no formal record.
Lacks give and take.	Allows for immediate response.
Appears impersonal and formal.	Is more personal, informal, and spontaneous.
Utilizes only one medium, print.	Usually encompasses two media, sound and nonverbal sight cues.[3]

To make a decision on media, you need to ask yourself these questions:

What are people supposed to do with the information?
How technical is the information?

---

[3] Sandra E. O'Connell, "The Information Connection," *Today's Secretary*, May 1975, p. 19.

How long is someone going to have to remember it?
How many people am I trying to reach?

Limit the Number of Ideas

You have determined your purpose and have selected the medium; the next step is to establish the parameters of your explanation. A parameter lets people know what you are and are not going to talk about. A data entry clerk needs to know the input process for the new on-line computer system. You do not have to give the history of data processing or even of that particular program. What you need to do is establish how and why the input system has changed, what the person needs to do, what results can be expected, and what to do in case of a problem.

By giving the parameters, you limit the scope and help the audience to know what to look for in your message. Parameters can be developed chronologically, by looking at functions, such as purchasing, research, and sales; or they can be given in amounts of money. Once you've determined the purpose, a topic may have built-in boundaries. Parameters can also vary depending on how much time you have available. One of the worst mistakes is to try and explain too much in too little time. You are better off explaining one thing clearly than many things not at all. How much time is available? To whom are you speaking? What do you want them to do with the information?

With this preparation behind you, begin the explanation by outlining the main points. Select those items which are crucial and group them together. If you can spend a few minutes preparing your explanation, write down all the points you want to cover. Your list may have ten or 12 items on it. Now examine the list, see what items might be grouped together, and put them in order of priority. Do some of the items relate to each other or are they out of order? Are there really two issues here instead of 12? Most people simply do not remember ten to 15 points; what *they* will remember are two or three main issues.

Example   You have a new vacation policy. People are allowed to carry days over into the second quarter of the year rather than losing them at the end of the year. There are a few exceptions to this policy, relating to length of service and job level.

How are you going to explain this to your employees?

Identify how the policy is different from the old policy, and then enumerate each difference.

Discuss exceptions; the policy applies except in particular cases. Delineate the sets of exceptions that exist.

What it comes down to is identifying the two major blocks of information and putting the explanatory material in this framework.

Use Language with a Common Frame of Reference

Try explaining to a stranger how to get to your office. You will find that certain landmarks and points of reference are so familiar to you that a stranger may get lost using your directions. Our frame of reference, our bank of experiences, is at the core of meaning. Chapter 1 presented the concept that meaning lies within the individual and is based in the person's experiences. Specialized language is built into nearly every field of work. Bankers, computer specialists, contractors, government employees, and manufacturers each have their own language. As a manager you must remember that other people may not understand your language. The problem is especially acute in technical fields, as highlighted by this comment in *Computerworld*.

> Communication problems are exacerbated in our case by the lack of a common language between user and analyst. The things with which we analysts work—specifications, data format descriptions, flowcharts, code, disk and core maps—are totally inappropriate for most users.
>
> The one aspect of the system the user is most comfortable talking about is the set of human procedures that are his interface to the system, typically something we don't get around to discussing in great detail with him until well after analysis, when the user manuals are being written.[4]

Even without the barriers of technical language, an explanation may be difficult to follow. Take, for example, the order, "Do the priority cases first." Unless the word "priority" has been clearly defined, the worker may select the wrong cases and thus not follow directions.

Language which is descriptive—that is, which refers to specific events and actions—is the most useful. (Descriptive language is discussed in more detail in Chapter 5.) Ask yourself what the words will mean to your audience, how might they be interpreted other than how you intended. Using feedback to check out meaning is a helpful technique in giving explanations.

---

[4] Tom De Marco, "Breaking the Language Barrier, Part I," *Computerworld*, August 7, 1978, p. 55.

Include Transitions and Summaries

Transitions serve as signposts to alert the listener to what's coming next. Summaries provide a review and highlight major issues. The signposts on the road tell you when there's a sharp turn ahead or a curve, allowing you to anticipate and adjust your behavior. Your reflexes are ready; you are more alert. Perhaps you slow down. Perhaps you speed up. Whatever, signposts act as a transition, allowing you to concentrate your energy and be prepared to give the appropriate response.

In oral as well as written communication, transitions aid the audience. Don't overlook the fact that most of us simply do not and cannot listen for long (or even short) periods of time. You may well say, "It's the listener's fault because the person is not tuned in." That may be, but, as the explainer, you want to get as much of your message across as possible. It is up to you to provide the motivation and to help the audience listen.

Transitions allow the listener to know when you're moving from one topic to the other. The first type of transition is an overview which tells the listener how many issues will be covered and, briefly, what they are. Early in your explanation describe what the person is supposed to be listening for. Are there three issues, with two main points each? Is this going to be in chronological order or by geographical region?

A second type of transition is the introductory phrase which gives clues as to what's coming next to help focus the listener's attention. They help to establish a frame of reference for the next point—for example, "Let's move on to the services we provide, which will be explained in detail." You give a signal with this transition that a change in material is forthcoming. Contrasts can also be indicated in advance with an introductory phrase.

Some examples of transitions:

"*On the other hand*, there are three factors to look at as disadvantages."

"We have examined the future. Now let us look at the *implications* for our department."

"These are the new procedures. We are going to be looking at the *three key transactions* which take place."

"Using last year's sales as a bench mark, *let's move on to this year*."

"*In contrast* to federal agencies, our procedures will be as follows."

Transitions may seem minor, yet they help both you and the listener.

The listener is provided with information which is useful in following the sequence of ideas and supporting information. As the person giving the explanation, you are provided with material which keeps you organized and on track. Confusion and possible misinterpretation are minimized for everyone.

Summaries can serve both as a transition and as a closing statement. Internal summaries can be used after completing a major section of the explanation. A good summary reinforces the material covered, demonstrates relationships among the supporting examples and illustrations, and high-lights critical issues. The summary should not provide a complete review which only lengthens the explanation. Brevity is most appropriate.

At the conclusion of an explanation, restate your goal and briefly discuss how each major point you covered fits the goal. By remembering your summary, people should be able to recall the main points of your explanation. This frame of reference will help them to ask questions when necessary. Additionally a good summary can motivate people to take action.

Don't Overqualify the Information

"Perhaps you might want to consider giving this proposal some attention."

At first glance this statement may appear acceptable. Read the sentence aloud and listen carefully: "Perhaps," "Maybe," "It's a proposal," qualify the statement. The number of qualifiers makes one wonder if the manager has any confidence at all in his or her judgment.

Overqualifying is often a reflection of anxiety or tension. You may be uncertain of someone's response, feel uncertain about the information, or in particular situations, not feel very confident. When you lose self-esteem, it may be reflected in apprehension.[5] Personal apprehension influences your choice of language which, in turn, affects the other person's response. Inadvertently you are sending a message which says: "I'm not very clear about this," or "This isn't really important." Qualifiers are important in order to be accurate, but they must be used judiciously and not interfere with the clarity of your explanation.

Each of us, at one time or another, will ramble or think out loud. It

---

[5] James C. McCroskey, John A. Daly, Virginia P. Richmond, and Raymond L. Falcione, "Studies of the Relationship Between Communication Apprehension and Self-Esteem," *Human Communication Research*, Spring 1977, p. 274.

is not possible to be clearly organized *all* the time. It is vital, however, that the people you work with know the difference between your ramblings and explanations of actions to be taken. It is not uncommon for managers, particularly chief executives, to muse out loud, and find within the week that great resources and energy have been expended fulfilling a request which was only mild curiosity.

Let people know why you are giving an explanation and what you expect. If you want resources committed and action taken, be clear about it. In time most people learn when you mean something for immediate action, when you want an idea analyzed, and when you are simply expressing random thoughts. From time to time check out the assumptions in your explanations and examine the results you are achieving.

Allow for Feedback

"But I only followed *your* instructions."
"I thought you said the report was due *next* week."
"I didn't know I had to record *all* transactions."

Each of these comments reflects some inaccuracy or distortion in the explanation process. Such inaccuracies are costly in terms of both production and frustration which results from being misunderstood. The best way to assure a reasonable degree of accuracy is to encourage feedback. You must know what the other person heard and what meaning is being attached to your explanation. By encouraging people to respond to what is said or written, more accurate action can result.

Perhaps you are seeking feedback by asking, "Did you understand me?" or "Have you got it straight now?" Unfortunately, these questions are not likely to yield much usable information. The questions are closed and put the employee on the spot by implying you may not have given a clear explanation. Instead, seek a more specific response. For example:

"What is your understanding of how we will handle overtime next month?"
"Describe how you will implement the zero defects program in your unit."
"Let's review the critical dates in this project."
"For clarity, will you summarize what we've covered so far?"

In each case you are encouraging a specific response which will at least tell you what was heard, and perhaps, what was misunderstood or not stated clearly. You then have the opportunity on the spot to correct the message. This is the primary function of feedback, to get information and use it for correction.

In long explanations it is helpful to provide for periodic feedback at major junctures rather than waiting until the end. If someone is confused early on, that confusion may color all the points which follow. Your response to the feedback needs to be accepting and clarifying without being judgmental. One of the reasons why managers don't get feedback is that people learn it is not wanted or they are made to feel wrong or stupid for giving it. Managers who are proficient at getting feedback are usually aware of problems before they occur and are able to make good use of their time when explaining.

SUMMARY

As the link between the employee and the organization, managers explain policy, procedures, and work-related matters. Carrying out the work of the organization, from the chief officer to the clerk delivering mail, relies on clear explanations.

Effective explanations will have the following key points:

1. Have a clearly stated purpose.
2. Make use of appropriate media.
3. Limit the number of ideas to be covered.
4. Use language which has a common frame of reference.
5. Help the listener with transitions and summaries.
6. Do not include too many qualifiers.
7. Allow for feedback.

Start improving your explanations by evaluating what you are currently doing. You could have a small cassette recorder with you and later evaluate the explanation yourself. You must, of course, tell people you are using a tape recorder and allow them the choice of not being recorded. This protects the individual's right to privacy and can reduce suspicion. Be most cautious in taping when others are present. Otherwise you may hurt your credibility to the point that your skills won't matter at all.

A second techique is to evaluate your skills using the self-assessment inventory below. Self-perception is valuable and can help increase awareness of what we ought to be doing. However, self-perception is not always accurate; it is hard to observe our own behavior. More important is how others perceive your explanations. A brief questionnaire to gain this kind of feedback from your boss, peers, or those who report to you follows the inventory. If you use this questionnaire, look for patterns in the responses. If one person feels you do not give clear purpose statements and most others do, you may want to talk to the individual rather than change this skill. If four out of five people feel you do not encourage feedback, then you should examine your own behavior to determine what you do that may close if off.

Once you have a picture of how you come across as an explainer, you can zero in on the items which are important to you and most in need of improvement. Taking time to plan an explanation following the guidelines in this chapter should lead to improvement. You will need practice to make the skills a natural part of your behavior. Incorporate the self-assessment and feedback from others into your personal communication plan in Chapter 7.

SELF-ASSESSMENT OF GIVING EXPLANATIONS

Check the extent to which you think you do each of the following in giving explanations.

	Very Little	Little	Some	Great	Very Great
1. Frame a clear purpose for listeners.					
2. Consciously select the appropriate media.					
3. Put limits on the amount of material I want to cover.					
4. Use language with a common frame of reference.					
5. Provide transitions and summaries to help people follow me.					
6. Give appropriate qualifiers so action is clear.					
7. Encourage people to give me feedback.					

SELF-ASSESSMENT OF EFFECTIVENESS OF EXPLANATIONS

Check the extent to which each of the following usually occurs when I explain policies and procedures.

	Very Little	Little	Some	Great	Very Great
1. The purpose is clear.	——	——	——	——	——
2. I know what you want me to do with the information.	——	——	——	——	——
3. The explanation is in print when I need the spoken word.	——	——	——	——	——
4. The explanation is oral when I need something in writing.	——	——	——	——	——
5. Covers too much information at once.	——	——	——	——	——
6. Gives so many qualifiers I'm not sure what you mean.	——	——	——	——	——
7. Allows time for feedback and discussion.	——	——	——	——	——
8. Encourages me to ask questions.	——	——	——	——	——
9. Answers my questions clearly.	——	——	——	——	——

POLICY CHECKLIST

To determine those policies which you should be particularly familiar with, check how often you need to explain them. There is also space to evaluate if your information is accurate, up to date and complete.

	Very Seldom	Little	Some	Great	Very Great	Accurate	Up to Date	Complete
1. Job-related procedures								
2. Technical manuals								
3. Budget requirements								
4. Change in work procedures								
5. Government regulations which affect our business								
6. New products or services								
7. Vacation/time off								
8. Salary								
9. Benefits								
10. Retirement								
11. Safety								
12. Training opportunities								
13. Performance expectations								
14. Career opportunities								
15. Probation/termination								

CHAPTER 5
DISCUSSING EMPLOYEE
PERFORMANCE

I am becoming more and more convinced that performance appraisal is going to be the issue of the next decade. So much hinges on the ability of organizations to appraise performance effectively, and yet we know so little about how to do it. Almost every personnel action with respect to an individual—pay increases, promotions, even hiring—that an organization would like to take should stem from its view of the person's performance.[1]

This comment by Edward Lawler, one of the leading experts on compensation and performance appraisal, highlights the critical role of performance appraisal in most organizations. *How* performance is appraised, the *system* by which you determine the overall evaluation, is not the subject of this chapter. There are a number of approaches for measuring performance; each organization needs to design a system to meet its own requirements. An effective performance appraisal system will measure job-related behaviors and not personality traits.[2]

No matter what system you use, at some point the appraisal becomes a conversation with the employee. And you, in turn, will be part of a conversation with your boss. Communication skills are particularly important in both these conversations. This chapter is designed to in-

---

[1] Ernest C. Miller, "Administering Pay Programs.... An Interview with Edward E. Lawler, III," *Compensation Review,* First Quarter, 1977, p. 9

[2] For approaches to performance appraisal systems see: David Ewing W. ed. *Performance Appraisal Series,* Harvard Business Review, #21143. Also Richard W. Beatty and Craig E. Schneier, *Personnel Administration: An Experiential Skill-Building Approach* (Reading, Mass.: Addison-Wesley, 1977).

crease the options available to you in conducting performance reviews and to reduce the chance of triggering defensive reactions. Regular performance discussions and ongoing performance feedback are key components of integrative communication. How you are doing on the job, and what career opportunities exist, heavily influence the perception of yourself and relationships in the organization.

WORK ENVIRONMENT AND PERFORMANCE REVIEW

For some time behavioral scientists have taken the position that ongoing feedback and regular review are important factors in motivation and productivity. The real thrust for performance review, however, has come from the government and the enforcement of EEO regulations. The laws regarding equal employment assure equal treatment on the job and equal access to promotion. As a result of the Supreme Court decision in *Grigg et al. v. Duke Power*, performance appraisal was given the same interpretation as employment tests. This means that performance rating instruments have to be derived from careful job analysis and based on information collected and scored under standardized conditions. Arbitrary, unchallenged, casual decisions on performance are simply not acceptable. The supervisor's decision has to be backed by a sound performance appraisal process.[3] Promotions, transfers, probationary actions, and termination of employment should all be done with great care in fairness to the employee. Documentation of such actions is needed for all concerned—employees, management, and the government. An objective system that makes an effort to review an employee's work—not color, personality, sex, or style of dress—is key to fair employment practices and is good business as well.

> A performance-based personnel system for selecting, utilizing, and developing corporate human assets should be—but rarely is—as much a component of sound business planning as financial, manufacturing, and market planning are. . . . Many decisions relating to people are not adequately concerned with performance, so managers lose control over quality of input, personnel expense, and resource development. . . . Even apart from the relevance to sound business practice, the hard fact is that government equal employment guidelines do treat the employment and development process as a system. . . . In treating these various steps as a

---

[3] William H. Holley and Hubert S. Feild, "Performance Appraisal and the Law," *Labor Law Journal*, July, 1975, pp. 423–430.

single system, the enforcement agencies impose some order on the fragmented, frequently chaotic, processes that usually characterize the management of an organization's greatest single investment.[4]

Additional legal impetus for systematic performance review comes from the retirement law which went into effect January 1, 1979. The vast majority of employees can now opt to work until age 70.

The new retirement law still allows dismissal for cause, but a case has to be built long before the ax falls. Developing that case will require a regular system of performance appraisal—normal in some companies but spotty or nonexistent in others. It is a safe bet that such formal evaluations will eventually become a commonplace of corporate life.[5]

If your system is designed only to meet government regulations and does not consider the organization's needs or those of the employee, it will probably not be very effective. The communication will be restricted because of the limited purpose: "This is just for the records."

The second reason for the expanding role of performance appraisal is the makeup of the work force. Organizations are now hiring people who were raised during the communication revolution. Employees who were born in the late 1950s and early 1960s are used to getting information immediately via television, satellite, and transisitor radio. Instantaneous access to information builds a mental set in which individuals expect to get the information they want when they want it. Carrying this behavior over to the job means that people expect to know how they are doing, where they may expect to go in the future, and (it is hoped) what can be done to improve chances of achieving personal goals. Employees are eager to control their own destinies and, much less inclined to accept lack of information in the 1980s than they were in past decades.

Third, managers are realizing that knowledge of work standards and level of performance is important to productivity. As we begin to understand the complexities of motivation, it has become apparent to researchers that feedback is vital to performance improvement. We all need to know how others see our work and whether or not it is measur-

[4] Herbert P. Froehlich and Dennis A. Hawver, "Compliance Spinoff: Better Personnel Systems," in *EEO: Avoiding Compliance Headaches,* (ed.) John M. Roach (New York: American Management Associations, 1973), pp. 17–18.
[5] Irwin Ross, "Retirement at Seventy: A New Trauma for Management," *Fortune,* May 8, 1978, p. 110.

ing up to their expectations. You may call this enlightened self-interest or good management. Whatever the label, there is gradual recognition that good performance appraisal is beneficial to the organization as well as to the employee.

The concern for employee rights is also part of the environment in which performance appraisal occurs. Employee rights include issues other than performance, such as unethical practices and political views. Traditionally an employee can object to a company policy at any time, and can also be fired for so doing. Those who favor more rights and freedoms for employees seek to protect the individual against retaliation from arbitrary and unethical bosses.[6] A clear record of performance, thoroughly and openly discussed, is one way to provide for employee rights and management prerogatives.

The social and political climate is moving toward more openness; to know what is expected on the job, how performance is being measured, and how one is doing. Government regulations, the communication revolution, and employees' rights all contribute to the growing need for effective performance discussions.

Recent communication research from over 20 organizations found that employees want more information on how they are being judged. Asked to rate the amount of information they received for "How you are being judged," on a five-point scale (1 = very little, 2 = little, 3 = some, 4 = great, 5 = very great), the average score for 5000 employees was 2.96.[7] When asked how much they would like to receive, employees answered that they wanted a great deal of information, a mean score of 4.06.

The social and political environment demands it, organizations need it, and employees want it. Yet you are not unusual if you find it difficult to discuss performance. When asked how they felt about holding performance discussions, managers have said:

"A delicate process."
"Scary."
"I don't like playing God."
"I don't want to hurt someone's feeling."
"It's hard; no one likes to hear negative feedback."

Talking to someone about his or her performance is an intimate conversation, because it affects so much of the person's life. Most people find it difficult to give negative feedback; it is particularly chal-

---

[6] David W. Ewing, "What Business Thinks About Employee Rights," *Harvard Business Review*, September–October 1977.
[7] Unpublished data, International Communication Association Audit, 1977 norms.

lenging to do so in a way which will result in improved performance. It is also difficult to talk to a good performer when there are few options for progress in the person's career. Even people who have moved upward in an organization can be frustrated because they feel further development is restricted by the lack of discussion of their performance. There are difficulties built into the appraisal situation that managers and supervisors are not necessarily equipped to handle. A study in two insurance conpanies showed that the performance appraisal discussion required a high degree of interview skills that most supervisors do not develop through experience.[8]

All the communication skills discussed in earlier chapters come into play in performance discussions: the style you choose; your paralanguage, symbolic, and nonverbal language; and the clarity of your explanations. This chapter covers the five skills most important to this particular communication: planning the discussion, describing behavior, responding to feelings, asking questions, and listening.

PLANNING THE DISCUSSION

The performance appraisal discussion lends itself well to planning. You know in advance when it will be held, you may have a company form to follow, and you have evidence of the individual's performance.

The first managerial step is to plan a performance review schedule for all the employees in your unit. Your organization may require annual, semiannual, or even quarterly reviews. Semiannually is most effective for many employees. Once you have a schedule, you can determine in advance how much planning time you will need. You should start about two weeks before the review is to take place. Allow one and one-half to two hours of preparation per employee.

In order to evaluate performance, you first have to have work standards. How much should the person be doing? Some jobs lend themselves more to quantitative measurement than others. If you already have work standards, an important part of the appraisal process is complete. If not, you will need to develop them.

> How many audits of what complexity can an auditor do in six months?
> What is the acceptable level of error on a production job?
> What are your service standards for handling customer calls?

---

[8] *The Components of Effective Performance Appraisal,* Life Office Management Association, Special Release No' 5, p. 15.

Without standards for each job, you will have difficulty describing performance expectations to the employee. Even if they have not been spelled out, most managers at least have an implicit notion of standards. You need to make the standards explicit so that employees can be told the expectations.

Once the desired level of performance is defined, you can then describe the employee's current performance. Specific information is required at this point. It can be obtained by observing, reading, quarterly reports, production runs, records of service, or other data from within the organization. In addition you should keep your own records providing examples of particularly good or bad performance. Known as a critical incident file, this is a notation of the details concerning a specific situation. You can keep such notes in each employee's file or in another appropriate place, as long as they are accessible (and decipherable) at the time you need them. Take care to keep employee information in a confidential file to protect each person's right to privacy. Added to these records are your own observations from walking through the work area and from direct contact with the employee in meetings or other conversations.

One danger in not keeping records is that the most recent performance influences you unduly. The review may then have a "horns or halo" effect, depending on the nature of the most recent incident. It is also difficult to be specific when relying on general impressions. Don't fall back on your memory for such important data.

Opening Comments

"Come on in. How have you been, Joe? How's the golf game?"

How would you react to this friendly opening if you knew the reason for the meeting was to discuss your performance? Most people would be a little anxious or at least curious as to what was coming next. Then there would be the awkward moment when you must change the subject and "get down to business."

As an "icebreaker" the social comment is not very effective for performance appraisals. You do need, however, to pay careful attention to the opening of the conversation. The first few minutes should help the person to understand the purpose of the review, your expectations for the meeting, and that you would like him or her to talk freely. Whatever your own approach, a sincere "icebreaker" is a good communication technique. A brief dialogue, perhaps, will help relax both you and the employee, but it must be sincere. Too many managers use hollow or superficial "icebreakers." If you can't be natural with this technique, don't use it!

The conversation should be two-way, so it is important *not* to have a script. Otherwise, the employee may feel there is no opportunity for questions or discussion. The opening statements should be clearly framed so that the conversation is initiated with maximum opportunity for openness. Identify specific questions that would involve the employee early, or outline the points you will be covering.

Identify what you want to have as a result of this conversation. Improved performance? In what area? How will you know if you get it? A change in behavior? Of what kind? How will you know if the goal is achieved?

Summary of Planning Process

Your plan, then, includes objectives, definition of performance expectations, description of current performance, opening comments, and questions. One of the most important, yet difficult, skills is to provide accurate, specific, nondefensive descriptions of performance to the employee.

DESCRIBING PERFORMANCE BEHAVIOR

What to you is a "good employee?" Underline the words in the list below which you think describe the behavior of a good employee.

Works to best of ability
Consistent performance
Reliable
Efficient
Loyal to the company
Has initiative
Is self-motivated

The words in the list above are all inferences—that is, they don't tell us anything about the person's behavior, only what you have inferred. Describing an employee's behavior is central to holding an effective discussion. This section discusses the use of language and techniques you can employ to describe behavior. The central concept is the difference between language which is inferential and that which is descriptive.

Descriptive Language Tells About Events or Behavior

Inferential language tells us someone's reaction to a situation, but it does not say anything about actual events or behavior. If you have ever had an employee transferred into your unit, you were probably told a number of inferences: The person is "aggressive," "smart," or "reliable." This tells you how another supervisor has reacted to the employee, but you don't really know anything about this person's performance. Inferences have so many different meanings that they tend to generate disagreement and misunderstanding, and they can prevent a clear discussion of performance.

Descriptive language, on the other hand, talks about what the person did in a given context.

> "For the last year in a unit which required submitting reports on monthly intervals, Anne Mahoney completed work on time, used data gathered from other employees, and presented work results clearly."

This sentence tells you what Ms. Mahoney did. "Reliable" is an inference made on the basis of the available information. You can determine if you are using inferences by asking if your statement describes what the person did or your reaction to it. One of the purposes of performance appraisal is to define expectations, how the individual is doing in relation to those expectations, and identify needed improvements. Inferential language simply does not accomplish that task.

Descriptive Language Can Be Observed and Verified by Others

Since inferences are judgments, they cannot be observed and exist only in an individual's mind. For example, you cannot observe initiative. You can, however, observe someone who comes in early the day of an important meeting to check all the materials which will be used.

When language is descriptive, others can observe the behavior. The key question, again, is what is the person *doing*? You will likely be talking about completion of assignments, meeting priorities, and the like in the context of a specific job. If others are present and can watch the employee, it is likely they will observe the same behavior, although reaction to the behavior may vary.

> The employee takes work from someone else's desk when finished with own tasks (behavior).
> Pushy (manager A's inference)

Aggressive (manager B's inference)

Has initiative (manager C's inference)

The inferences tell you about the manager's values, not about the employee.

If you use language which is hard to verify, the discussion is wide open for disagreement and may trigger defensive or closed communication.

Manager: You're not showing enough responsibility.

Trainee: I feel I am showing responsibility.

Manager: But you let too many things slip by you.

The discussion becomes a hassle over the inference. If, instead, you begin the discussion with a description of behavior, you have a stronger basis for gaining agreement on the actual level of performance.

Agreement Is More Likely with Descriptive Language

The problems posed by inferential language can be easily demonstrated from your personal experience. When was the last time you went to a movie or restaurant highly recommended by a friend and were sadly disappointed?

"This movie is terrific."

"Really, I thought it was terrible."

"How could you think that? She is such a great actress."

"But I've always hated her pictures."

The language generates disagreement because you do not have a common point of reference. Unless you are very sure based on past experience what your friends mean by, "This is a terrific movie," you should not take their inference—nor any inference—at face value.

When a discussion is opened with inferential language, you are likely to get disagreement or at best not know what the agreement means. When you are descriptive, the person knows your point of reference.

"The reports in the last quarter were two days late, did not contain all the budget information, and lacked recommendations for action."

Agreement will not necessarily be automatic, but the language gives a clear description of behavior and provides a realistic basis for discussion.

Descriptive Language Is Specific and Concrete

"You have a lousy attendance record."
"You have been late two times a week for the last five weeks. Our standard is two latenesses per quarter."

Your choice of the word lousy is sure to get the employee thinking of excuses, feeling attacked, and not willing to discuss behavior. The second example is clearer and more specific, although not necessarily more pleasant. The person may still try to think of reasons why, depending on what you say next, but at least both of you know what behavior occurred and what is expected.

Language is the process of assigning symbols for our experience; it cannot *completely* represent all that can be said about a person's behavior. For efficiency we leave out details and develop shorthand in our conversations.

This concept has been described as a ladder of abstraction.

Inferential   John won't make it in this organization.

                  John won't make it in this department.

                  John isn't very smart.

                  John doesn't know the products.

                  John was inaccurate with the sales representative.

                  John spoke with a sales representative and gave inaccurate product information on the new copying
Concrete   equipment last Tuesday.

As you move down the ladder of abstraction, there is a progressive addition of detail. Each statement tells us more about John's behavior. How much detail you use will depend on your past relationship with the person and how much you trust your communication experience. Most managers use less detail than is appropriate in performance discussions.

When you are concrete and specific rather than abstract and general, the employee has a better chance of being open with you and ready to solve the problem and improve performance. "You're careless with the customers," doesn't tell John anything about his behavior and makes it difficult for him to perform differently.

Descriptive Language Uses Action Verbs

> Susan is smart.
> Fred was a good worker.
> Lillian is efficient.
> Ken is helpful.

The verb "is" makes it sound as if these people possess some inherent quality or capacity, such as "smart." The verb "is" also keeps us from understanding the basis for the judgment. People are not "lazy." Rather in given circumstances they perform tasks with varying degrees of skill and efficiency. When describing behavior, forms of the verb to be—was, has, is, are—are signs that you are using inferential language. Language is more likely to be descriptive when action verbs are used.

> John *wrote* a complete report: It *contained* all the unit figures for production, analyzed costs by product, and *included* projections for next year.

Notice that forms of the verb "to be" are missing from this sentence. We often need the "is" inferences in our informal conversation, but in performance appraisal action verbs provide clarity and a basis for understanding.

Descriptive Language Is Qualified Rather than Absolute

Language is often used to categorize people ("He is a poor performer.) implying an absoluteness and finality about the person. This statement is a reflection of personal standards and does not reveal much about the employee. The personal judgment becomes a "fact," rather than a description of the person. Using absolute language ignores the differences among employees and tends to stress the similarities.[9] Language which is absolute is characterized by traits, qualities that force a diagnosis of the individual's personality. The differences among people are a more fruitful matter for discussion. The traits often used in performance appraisal forms, such as leadership, initiative, team effort, and reliability, may force you into this kind of diagnosis, but this is hardly the function of performance appraisal. If such traits appear on the forms you use, be sure not to use them in the discussion unless you can be very clear and descriptive as to the meaning of those terms.

A person may be a poor performer in a job which calls for coordination with other units, yet does very well in a job which requires sta-

---

[9] Wendell Johnson, *People in Quandries* (New York: Harper & Row, 1946), p. 208.

tistical reports. The label "poor performer" has the quality of absolute-ness, as if in all situations, at all points in time, the person is a poor performer.

Qualifiers, on the other hand, allow you to be more descriptive and generally refer to time, place, and context. "You *always* come to staff meetings late." It's possible that observation would show this to be true. For most situations, though, "always" is extreme. And in this particular conversation, "always" will trigger feelings of being trapped and a de-sire to defend with, "Last week I was there on time." *Always* and *nev-er* are examples of absolutes which should be avoided in performance discussion. Instead, refer to the job standards, the conditions of the work assignment, and the specific context of the performance. Use qualifiers such as "the last six months," and "doing programming with FORTRAN" Qualifiers add to the clarity and accuracy of your de-scription.

Descriptive Language Is Relatively Free of Value Judgment

Descriptive language tells what happened with little connotation of judgment. Yet a performance appraisal ultimately is a managerial judgment which you must be prepared to make. Strategically it is bet-ter to use descriptive language first so that the basis for the judgment is clear.

"You are not listening to your people."
"You are a poor supervisor."

These statements do not tell the supervisor anything about his or her behavior, or what to do differently. If you want performance im-proved, language which is relatively value free would be more helpful. Some possibilities:

The people in your unit were not aware of the change in work hours which we discussed at the staff meeting last week.
The work in your unit does not get done when you are out or away at a meeting.
The trainees are not aware of the new work which was assigned to your area last week.

These sentences describe specific behaviors which, if agreed upon, can be used to develop plans for improvement. "Be a better supervisor," can be interpreted in an infinite number of ways, leading to misunderstanding and another low evaluation of supervisory skills the next review.

Descriptive Language Does Not Attribute Motives

In our culture, with its "pop" psychology, many of us have taken to instant analysis of what motivates others. The fact is, we don't *really* know motives, unless someone tells us. Even then, their reason may not be accurate or completely clear. Telling others what their motives are is presumptuous, often contributes to closed communication, and it is ineffective for several reasons:

> It makes many assumptions which could be inaccurate.
> Most of us feel put upon by such analysis.
> It closes communication and makes full analysis of causes difficult.

If you have already decided on the reasons for behavior, the person being reviewed may feel it is pointless to tell you another side of the situation.

> "You are not interested in your work."
> "You are afraid of responsibility."
> "You lack initiative."

These motives may or may not be operating, nor is it relevant whether they are or not. What's important is how the employee sees the situation and what you can do about it. If the employee is able to identify lack of interest as a reason for poor performance, then you can analyze the situation together. Determine what might be done on the job to make the work more interesting, what development is available, what opportunities there are in the company, or possibly, elsewhere if it's better for the person to leave.

Summary of Descriptive Language

Language is seldom either purely inferential or purely descriptive, but rather it possesses some degree of both. Inferential–descriptive language can be placed on a continuum with degrees, allowing you to choose the degree of description which is appropriate to the situation.

Inferential	Descriptive
tells about how other person feels	tells about the event
cannot be observed or verified	can be observed and verified
agreement is difficult	agreement easier
uses the verb "to be"	uses action verbs
allness/absolutes	includes qualifiers
general/abstract	concrete/specific
value judgment	free of values
attributes motives	open to alternative motives

Review these concepts and look at the sentences below.

"You are a poor listener."
"You could do better if you would try harder."
"You always rush into my office with the tough decisions you haven't thought through."

In the first sentence we have two problems: use of "are" (verb to be) and a value judgment ("poor"). A more accurate statement would be: "You interrupted me three times in the last five minutes." The second sentence implies a motive, that poor work is caused by not trying hard enough. A description of behavior would be: "Your work in the last three months shows you understand and can sell half of our products. Knowing all our products would be useful in doing complete customer service." The third statement contains an absolute, a value judgment, and a motive. It is almost certain to trigger some kind of defensive behavior. An alternative: "Last month there were many decisions to be made on the flow of materials to the production line. On five occasions you asked me to make the decision. When I asked for your view, you did not have all the data available and had not analyzed the cause of bottlenecks."

Descriptive statements do take a bit longer than the quick categorical inferences. The time is well spent, however, as descriptions help the employee to understand your meaning and enable the two of you to identify behavior which can be changed.

The sentences below each contain several inferences. Use the work of your unit to write a descriptive statement.

1. You need to learn to manage your people better.
1a. _____
2. Your technical work is not up to par because you just don't care.
2a. _____

RESPONDING TO THE EMPLOYEE[10]

In addition to the important job of describing performance standards and actual performance, much of the discussion will center on responding to the employee. Many of the anxieties which managers experience in this situation stem from concern over how to respond.

> "What will I do if the person gets hostile?"
> "How do I handle someone who is closed and doesn't accept criticism?"
> "What can I do when someone simply won't talk?"

All these questions are seeking ways to respond to the employee which will be satisfying and lead to improved performance. There are three concepts which can be of help to you: self-management, question asking, and active listening. Taken together, skills in each of these areas will equip you to manage well in most performance reviews.

Self Management

Before thinking about how to respond to another person, you need to be aware of your own feelings and behavior. Performance review systems should identify objective standards for jobs. Yet an element of subjectivity remains. You are, as a manager, asked to make judgments and communicate them. Knowing your own feelings and how you respond to others can help you select appropriate responses. Anticipating how the other person *may* react can be useful to you in planning the communication. Be cautious in your analysis, but at least think about how the employee has reacted in the past, the degree to which he or she can express ideas and feelings, and willingness to ask questions. The trap in such anticipation is that you may make unwarranted assumptions. You may want to role play the conversation in your head: Make a statement, listen to the reply, then examine your own response to see the direction the communication will take from there.

---

[10] Material in this section was developed with Sheldon Hughes, Organization Development Consultant.

For example, your senior technician disagrees with most of your description. Disagreement can be reduced, of course, by using descriptive language. The employee's questions or disagreement may be generated by the inferences you used. How do you react when someone appears angry, defensive? Each of us responds differently. Some get angry and shout, others withdraw, and some get frustrated or disgusted. These feelings may trigger you into responses which are not helpful to the conversation. This is not to say that your responses may be inappropriate, only that you want to be aware and select responses during the conversation. If you are frustrated, ask why. If you have been over the same ground several times before, your frustration is understandable. The question is why performance hasn't improved. Did the person know what specific behavior you expected? You may have set off some of the defensive behavior by your communication. Perhaps personal difficulties are interfering with the employee's ability to listen. You cannot be responsible for everyone's personality, only for the clarity of your own communication.

Be Firm with Negative Feedback

Monitoring your feelings does not mean backing away from negative feedback. Telling people their performances are inadequate (even with descriptive language) is difficult. Your feelings of discomfort in this situation may lead you to waiver, to overqualify or downplay the importance of the behavior. If the employee disagrees, point out specific examples. Be open to new information, but do not avoid confronting the individual with less than satisfactory performance.

For example, feeling uncomfortable telling people they have turned in work that was inaccurate 40 percent of the time could make you say "This isn't too important" or "I don't want you to get too upset about this." These messages may lead the employee to think the behavior does not need to be changed.

Being aware of your feelings should help you to select appropriate responses and to be firm and clear when needed.

There are three considerations in managing yourself:

1. Be aware of your own reactions.
2. Evaluate the intensity and appropriateness of your reaction.
3. Select appropriate communication behavior which will help achieve your goals.

A manager, aware of feelings and reactions, is able to think, "I am getting frustrated because this person doesn't seem to be listening."

Knowing feelings is the first step in selecting appropriate behavior. We may try to ignore the feeling, only to have it come out in tone of voice, impatience in body language, or a snap decision. You do not necessarily express the feeling to the employee, although you may well do so.

It is not always necessary to trust your feelings, as not all feelings are trustworthy guides to behavior.[11] Some feelings mask others and prevent us from knowing what we are really feeling. Feeling anxious about firing someone is an understandable and predictable response. If you completely trusted the feeling of anxiety, you might decide not to terminate employment even though all your experience and data say you should. This feeling may be a mask for another feeling, the conversation may be unpleasant, and most people are uncomfortable in taking such a severe action. Trusting the feeling could lead you away from appropriate action.

Acknowledging what you are feeling in response to the employee does not necessarily mean you will act on the feeling, only that you are in tune with yourself. With this information, you can then evaluate the feelings to help determine a response. Is your reaction based on this interview with this employee? Or are you disappointed over a proposal which was turned down at a recent meeting? Although it may be difficult, try to focus on this one employee during the discussion. In evaluating your response, consider how the employee may react. Some people will respond well when you ask questions; others will not.

Selecting appropriate behavior means using the question asking and active listening skills.

ASKING QUESTIONS

Asking effective questions is a skill that can be acquired. Discussions often become defensive and closed because the manager is unaware of the impact of questions. The three types of questions you need to be aware of during performance appraisal are direct, open, and clarifying.

Direct Questions

These questions are designed to:

Gather specific information
Give the other person an idea of what you want to know

---

[11] James Elliott, "When Not To Trust Your Feelings," *Personal Growth*, No. 23.

Eliminate misunderstanding of what answer is required
Guide the discussion toward a specific problem

Direct questions are very useful when you are trying to find how an event occurred, exactly what the other person did. Some examples are:

"Did you go to the training class?"
"What are the causes of the time delays?"
"What data did you use to do the budget?"
"Who did you contact to find out about the retirement benefits?"

Each of these can be answered with a phrase, or even a yes or no. Direct questions can be limiting, in that the responder may supply brief information when you needed an extended answer. "Did you go to the training class?" will tell you whether or not the person attended the class, but it is not a good question if you are trying to find out what the individual learned. Direct questions can be used when the responder has the specific information available, has used inferences that are not clear to you, or has a hard time participating in a discussion.

Direct questions may limit the communication because they can make you sound like an attorney conducting a cross-examination. Also, depending on your paralanguage, the other person can feel attacked and become defensive. "Who wrote this report?" can be delivered in a tone which suggests a compliment, a threat, or is simply asking for a name. It is the combination of tone of voice and stress on words which changes the meaning. If used too frequently or with someone who is unprepared to answer, direct questions will be counterproductive and result in less rather than more information.

Open Questions

Open questions are designed to get a wide range of answers and require several sentences or more in reply. We use open questions when seeking an opinion, an explanation of how something is done, reasoning behind an action, or attitudes and feelings. They are useful in that they give the employee more control over the conversation.

Get information without creating defensiveness.
Allow the person to express a personal point of view.
Leave room for the conversation to branch.
Gather additional information.

Open questions are characterized by several introductory phrases:

"How do you see . . .?"

"What's your view . . .?"
"What do you think . . .?"
"How do you feel . . .?"

Managers often see a need for this kind of information but ask for it in a circuitous way: "Do you think that you made a poor selection on the last hire?" That question tells the person what to think and is not really open or seeking an opinion. Another favorite seems to be, "Don't you feel that it would be in your best interest to . . .?" That is not a question but a statement. When you want to make a statement, do so openly; don't hide it as a question. Whenever you insert the word "that" after your first few words, it's likely you have a statement hiding as a question. Most of us recognize questions masquerading as statements and resent this form of manipulation. The answers then are not necessarily honest, but geared to what is wanted.

Open questions are very useful in performance reviews. This is one conversation where the employee's view is terribly important. If any behavior change is going to occur, the employee has to agree with the perception of the problem, be able to supply information to analyze the causes, or identify career aspirations. In each of these cases, open questions are your key to getting this kind of information.

An employee has agreed to being dissatisfied with the work. The question might be: "What jobs in our area interest you?" Or the person disagrees with your evaluation of writing skills. An open question might be: "How do you evaluate your writing skills?"

As helpful as they are, open questions are not without limits. Conversations can get sidetracked, you can become overloaded with more information than you need, or the employee may simply find it difficult to respond. Open questions require some thought, so don't be afraid to let a few moments of silence go by before you get a response.

Clarifying Questions

When you need more information, you need to ask a clarifying question. The purposes of clarifying questions are to:

Promote full information
Help prevent misunderstandings
Clarify points that have been made
Ensure that the meaning of the words expressed is understood

Most of us know how to ask clarifying questions, but miss opportunities to do so. One important clue to watch for is when the other person has used inferential language. Since you need to know what the inference is based on, you can ask for more information in a variety of ways.

"Tell me more about that."

"Give me some examples."

"How did you arrive at that decision?"

"You said you have problems all the time with the copying clerk. Would you be more specific?"

These questions encourage the responder to talk more, to elaborate, and to provide you with needed details. Clarifying questions, too, have their difficulties. If used too often, they may lead to a belief that you're not listening. They can be time-consuming, and if you are not prepared to take the time, you can give the impression it was a futile exercise. And an employee may find it hard to respond if the topic or problem has not been thought through ahead of time.

Loaded Questions

There is a fourth category of questions—loaded questions—and these should be avoided. A question which is loaded has a hidden agenda or an implied answer. Loaded questions tend to back people into a corner and make them feel they have to justify their actions. Your sense of "winning" may be helped, but loaded questions are not conducive to solving problems.

"Don't you agree that you missed the deadline because of poor planning?"

"You won't find yourself in this predicament again, will you?"

"Wouldn't you agree it's your responsibility to check all the information before it goes out?"

If you want to make these comments, then do so honestly and with straightforward statements. "I think you missed the deadline because your planning wasn't comprehensive enough." Most people sense when they are being set up with a loaded question and feel frustrated or angry because the question does not leave them free to respond openly. The employee knows you are seeking a particular answer and may agree only to terminate this portion of the discussion. Thus agreement has not really been reached, and positive action is not likely to result.

Summary

You will have the opportunity during most reviews to ask a variety of questions. To select the type which is most appropriate, first identify what you want to know, then, knowing the other person, decide the best way to achieve that purpose.

Say you want to know what occurs when a supervisor delegates, because you believe he or she is not delegating enough of the technical work. After each question in the list below, check the category which identifies the type of question.

	Direct	Open	Clarifying	Leading
1. You're not delegating much, are you?	_____	_____	_____	_____
2. What has happened in the past when you delegated projects?	_____	_____	_____	_____
3. You said your people are too busy. What kind of work are they doing?	_____	_____	_____	_____
4. Tell me what you do when you do delegate?	_____	_____	_____	_____
5. What happens when you do delegate?	_____	_____	_____	_____
6. What are the top three priorities in your unit this month?	_____	_____	_____	_____
7. Who do you have that could handle the budget work?	_____	_____	_____	_____
8. What does delegation mean to you?	_____	_____	_____	_____

Question 1 is leading and is likely to produce a defensive reaction. Questions 3, 4, and 8 are open, searching for opinions, meanings, and points of view. Questions 6 and 7 are direct, looking for specific information, and questions 2 and 5 are clarifying, probing for follow-up details.

One category of question is not necessarily better than another; it is best to select the type of question which will get the result that you need. Learning to hear yourself, as with all communication behavior, is the important first step in selecting appropriate questions. If you are like most managers, you are asking more loaded questions than you realize, and may be using direct questions when you would get more information with open questions.

ACTIVE LISTENING

Performance appraisal, perhaps more than any other conversation, should be an interactive process. That means that both participants need to be good listeners, which is certainly an abstraction. Good listening is so widely accepted as an important management behavior that we don't need to discuss its validity. Yet, in practice, what is a manager doing when being a good listener? The four primary behavioral components of good listening are clarifying questions, paraphrasing, reflecting, and nonverbal responsiveness.

Clarifying Questions

We have just discussed the types of questions available to you. Clarifying questions, used judiciously, are a way to show you heard what was just said. You recognize the other person's comments and are interested enough to want to know more, which can function as an important way of confirming the other person.

Paraphrasing

Paraphrasing involves restating in a brief way what you heard the other person say. It refers to content, not to feelings which are discussed below under reflecting. "What I hear you are saying, then, is. . . ." "Your main interests are in working with people and new ideas." Paraphrasing is an important skill to check on your own listening. We think we heard accurately, but can't really be sure until it is checked with the orginator. This technique can help keep the conversation from going astray, with each participant operating from a different meaning and each assuming knowledge of what was meant. Paraphrasing can also be used to get the conversation back on track if you have wandered into tangential issues. It is especially important at the close of an interview so that both parties are clear as to what action plans were agreed to.

Reflecting Feelings

The intensely personal nature of the performance review means that feelings are likely to be expressed both directly and indirectly. You will find it helpful, especially when feelings are intense, to reflect how the person seems to be feeling. Acknowledging feelings openly is an important component of listening, as well as a way to demonstrate that you will accept feelings, confirm the individual, and open the communication. The examples below show how to make reflective comments.

"You're feeling pretty frustrated by the amount of overtime in the
    last month."

"You are unhappy because you don't see opportunity for promo-
    tion here."

"You're confused, then, as to what your role needs to be."

These statements are made *after* the employee has expressed something to you. Be careful not to tell the employee what to feel, only to
reflect back what is coming across to you. Some introductory phrases
can help: "Sounds like you feel. . . ." or "You seem to feel. . . ."

Each of these openings is designed to keep you accurate and honest, only reflecting back to the other person what you have observed.
Although reflecting feelings can trigger a further discussion which
could be quite emotional, it can also reduce the intensity of the feelings
simply by accepting them and allowing them to be expressed. The employee's feelings may not change when you make a reflective statement, but he or she may be better able to cope with them.

Nonverbal Responses

Your facial expression and body movement do provide a great deal of
information, often in ways not immediately apparent. If you are tap-
ping your fingers in impatience waiting for the other person to finish,
or looking away when a disagreement occurs, you may be saying, "I'm
not listening." This message gets translated as, "The boss doesn't think
I'm worth listening to," or, "Why did she ask that if she wasn't going to
pay attention?" Feigning interest when you are bored is a technique
mastered by nearly every school child, and it is not what I am suggesting. Only examine your behavior and think about its impact on others.
You may have ten performance reviews to do this quarter, but this is
the only one for that particular employee. You owe the person your
full attention. Each of us has our own style and body language; some
are more expressive than others. There are times to be impassive and
not let the other person know what you are thinking, but if you overdo
this response, your employees are likely to feel confused, hurt, and un-
clear as to your meaning.

Summary

There is much to be gained from developing the skills of good listening. First, you may find out something you did not know or had failed
previously to hear. Second, the other person will feel more confident
and open with someone who is genuinely interested and responsive.

Third, you are relieved of the burden of doing all the talking and encouraging participating in the evaluation.

SUMMARY

A performance review is a demanding discussion for both parties, requiring clarity and accuracy of communication, sensitivity to feelings, ability to solve problems, and the capacity to listen. The concepts and skills presented in this chapter can—with practice—greatly increase your competence in conducting these discussions. Yet communication skills are not the answer to every problem. There will be people who will not be able to talk very much, even with your open questions. Others may not be able to see the flaws in their performance, no matter how descriptive you are. Or if your organization does not have ways for you to reward outstanding performance, good communication will not overcome the frustration the employee may feel.

On balance applying the concepts of descriptive language, active listening, responding to feelings, and asking appropriate questions will lead to effective discussions. How can you tell if you are achieving the desired results?

First, look for improved performance by the individual. Reports which were late are now on time, a supervisor who didn't delegate is making more use of his or her people, the rejection rate of products is lower. Second, look for increased openness between you and the employee, demonstrated by more sharing of information and a willingness to discuss problems and feelings. Third, instead of feeling uncomfortable and apprehensive, you should feel competent and at ease in the performance discussion.

There will still be times when the review is difficult, but now you have a repertoire of skills from which to choose. Each person needs to be treated as an individual. That's why this chapter offers no formulas for successful interviews. Rather, you increase your kmowledge of what skills can be used, learn to hear yourself through the self-assessment test which follows, and select the skills you need to suit various situations. The case study below is intended to help you begin practicing these skills. Read the case, then use the questions for analysis to see how you would do under the circumstances described. The real test, of course, comes when you schedule, plan, and conduct reviews with the people who report to you. You needn't wait until a formal review to practice these skills. Giving performance feedback is an ongoing, almost daily, process for a manager. Start practicing and perfecting your skills today.

CASE STUDY

PERFORMANCE EVALUATION

You are going to hold a performance review with Alice Smith. She has been with the company for six years; she was promoted to supervisor after an outstanding record as a quality control analyst. She seems eager to get ahead and fulfills her technical responsibilities with great care.

In fulfilling her supervisory responsibilities you have noticed the following:

> She tends to rush in with solutions to problems before examining all aspects of the situation.
>
> Two new sets of procedures were implemented without planning and work has to be redone.
>
> Her follow-through on cases is uneven. Rush cases are not dealt with unless you check several times.
>
> She seems hesitant to push her people to get the work out on time.
>
> She prefers to deal with complex cases herself (at which she is good) but this makes it hard for her people to ask questions.

In a discussion three months ago you raised these issues. She felt that you wanted her to "sacrifice quality for quantity."

You feel that unless her supervisory functions are handled better that you can't afford to keep her in this position. You have asked Alice in for another performance discussion.

Analysis of Performance Evaluation

1. Underline the words in the case which are inferences.
2. Using your own work unit for the specifics, rewrite the inferences to be descriptive statements.
3. What are your own feelings in holding a discussion under these circumstances?
4. Which responses (based on your feelings) will be most helpful to the discussion?
5. Which responses might not be helpful?
6. Write out several questions which you could use to get more information from Alice.

7. Check the questions to see if they are direct, open, or clarifying.

8. What are the key performance issues? What specific behavior do you expect from Alice in the future?

9. Think of someone who works for you or that you have known in the past who could get this kind of performance evaluation. Now identify how that person might respond to receiving this information.

10. How will you handle this person's responses?

SELF-ASSESSMENT OF DISCUSSION SKILLS

Assess the level of your skills using the following scale:
1 = need work to acquire the skill; 2 = able to do—need to do more often; 3 = able to do—use effectively.

	1	2	3
1. Open the discussion effectively.			
2. Able to define expected results.			
3. Use concrete, descriptive language.			
4. Back up value judgments with clear standards.			
5. Use questions appropriately.			
6. Responsive to other person's feelings.			
7. Firm with negative feedback.			
8. Listen to other person's point of view.			
9. Not get "hooked" by negative responses.			
10. Paraphrase other person's statements.			

PERFORMANCE APPRAISAL FACTORS AND DEFINITIONS

The following descriptions are taken from the Michigan Credit Union League Performance Appraisal Program. To be usable in different parts of the organization, inferential factors are used. The definitions are moderate-level inferences which managers use as a guide to be even more descriptive in reviewing a specific employee.

Job Knowledge

Possesses information, skills and judgment required to perform (his/her) job with minimal assistance.

Knows where to find required information and how to use it.

Sufficient knowledge of job to solve problems of job with minimal reference to supervisor.

Understands procedures and workflow and how they relate to job.

Understands functional relationship of units and departments.

Understands and adheres to company policy.

Planning and Organization

Defines and meets realistic work goals.

Sets priorities, estimates time, monitors work, and anticipates problems.

Uses time effectively.

Work assignments are well planned.

Develops efficient systems and procedures.

Makes efficient use of all available resources.

Coordinates all areas of job/project.

Contribution to Team Effort

Proposes new ideas regarding goals, policies, and improved work procedures.

Takes initiative to achieve objectives when opportunities and problems arise.

Demonstrates cooperative spirit in working with others, both within and outside unit, department, and company.

Accepts changes with positive attitude.

Is receptive to constructive criticism; exchanges advice and opinions with others.

Takes initiative in improving work skills.

Contributes effectively to committee or task force assignments.

Reliability/Dependability

Completes assignments on or ahead of schedule.

Accepts responsibility for job and works with minimal supervision.

Can be relied upon to assist in rush assignments and special projects.

Meets company standards in attendance and punctuality.

Meets goals and objectives agreed upon in previous reviews.

CHAPTER 6
OPEN COMMUNICATION

General Electric has "Hotline"; at IBM, it's "Speak Up!" and "Open Door"; Atlantic Richfield has "ArcoSpeak"; Equitable Life Assurance employees can use "EquiVoice"; while Honeywell people go to "Inside Line"; Connecticut General calls it "Open Line"; and Xerox has an ombudsman.

All these are examples of upward communications programs. They provide a way for employees to ask questions, voice complaints, and have grievances heard. Organizations are finding it increasingly important to have a vehicle for upward communications. The reasons vary. People find it difficult to talk to their supervisor, management wants to find out what is on employees' minds, to dispel rumors, to provide an objective means for concerns and the addressing of grievances. In addition EEO compliance may require an upward communication program so that employees can try to resolve discrimination issues internally before seeking the help of an outside agency.

Upward communication programs take four basic forms: (1) an anonymous or signed column in the company newspaper; (2) a form which provides space for questions and gives a confidential response directly to the employee; (3) a hotline phone, or (4) an ombudsman or counselor. Each organization adapts one or more of these formats to its own structure, employee needs, and resources.

The effectiveness of these efforts at upward communication is not really known, because little formal research has been done. Success is usually defined in terms of how many people use the program. Since its inception in 1958, the IBM "Speak Up!" program handled 100,000

questions from employees. Organizations which have ombudsmen report success, yet the concept has not become widespread in industry.[1]

A recent study of *Fortune* 300 nonindustrials found that of 130 re-
spondents, 48 percent maintained some type of employee-management
communication program. The median number of annual inquiries
from employees was 200. The most significant achievements of the
programs according to their directors were:

1. Giving employees a sense that management is listening and
   wants their opinions;
2. Learning employee concerns;
3. Pointing out potential trouble areas which might be overlooked
   otherwise;
4. Providing a safety valve for employee frustration.

When asked to evaluate how employees perceive the upward communication program, the directors felt that the two most significant factors were the opportunity for employees to express their frustrations
and the opportunity to ask questions without fear of reprisal.[2]

We have little systematic knowledge as to what kinds of problems
have arisen, if and how they were resolved, or what employees think of
the organization's efforts at open communication.

Even if we acknowledge the success and importance of upward
communication programs, *they do not address the central issue* of how
to maintain open communication between managers or supervisors and
the people who report to them. An upward communication program is
not a substitute for an effective line manager. As the ombudsman at
Xerox commented, such a program cannot "replace the vital need for
an employee and his manager to be honest and open with each other."[3]

Third-party systems do have the advantage of neutrality, which is
important under some conditions. At the same time going outside the
defined chain of communication does not help the people who face
each other every day to communicate any better. In some cases, where
a counselor intervenes, improvement is possible, but the factors which
restricted communication in the first place are likely to remain. An alternative needs to be available to employees whose problems are not
satisfactorily dealt with in the line, but it is not a replacement for the
desired quality of communication. As stated in Chapter 1, communica-

[1] "Where Ombudsmen Work Out," *Business Week*, May 3, 1976, p. 114.
[2] Virginia Terry, "Upward Communication Programs Within United States Non-Indus-
trial Corporations," a study conducted through Occidental Life Insurance of California,
unpublished manuscript, 1978, pp. 40–44.
[3] *New York Times*, May 1, 1976.

tion is the process by which you manage. Therefore it is part of all your responsibilities, and it continuously affects daily actions. Communication with your employees is not the job of an ombudsman or a column in the company newspaper.

This chapter is about how to develop and maintain open communication between managers and the people who work directly for them. Barriers to open communication and ways to reduce those barriers are discussed. Underlying this chapter is the assumption that the communication which occurs daily between managers and their people is vital, while open-line communication programs are needed to assure fair treatment in large systems.

WHAT IT IS AND IS NOT

In these days of books which "tell all," popular psychology which advocates openness and confrontation, and the adage, "Let it all hang out," the term "open" communication needs definition in an organizational context. We would do well to keep in mind this comment from psychiatrist Willard Gaylin, "I have never felt that people's inner feelings have some claim to public recognition."[4] In the workplace, open communication is the *mutual* sharing of information and feelings, freedom to disagree and ask questions, and the expectation of information about matters which affect you and your responsibilities *at work*.

Open communication involves both telling and listening. Being informed of changes and the reasons for them is an act of telling; trying to understand the reasons and being receptive to the change is an act of listening. Open communication is different from upward communication in that it is mutual, including telling and listening on both sides. Rather than upward or downward communication, which is unilateral, open communication emphasizes mutuality and receptivity of both parties, no matter what their level in the organization. Upward communication is usually thought of as the need of nonmanagement people to express views to management. Studies have shown, however, that managers have the same needs for more open channels.[5] Several of the upward communication programs have found that managers use the program as much as nonmanagement personnel.

In open communication a distinction can be made between the sharing of ideas and the sharing of feelings. Generally people in organi-

---

[4] Willard Gaylin, M.D. *Feelings: Our Vital Signs* (New York: Harper & Row, 1979), p. 4.
[5] W. Charles Redding, *Communication Within the Organization* (New York: Industrial Communication Council, 1972), p. 364.

zations do better (although not always) sharing ideas than sharing feelings. Ideas are relatively objective and impersonal, while feelings are subjective and personal. The expression of ideas or thoughts is "safe" while expressing feelings involves more risk and can make a person more vulnerable.

Idea	*Feeling*
We didn't get our output because the computer was down.	I'm really ticked off at the systems department.
We need a new drill press to complete the job.	I don't understand why this company is so foolish as to not maintain the equipment.
I think we ought to try recruiting at the community colleges.	I'm really excited about the possibilities of my idea.

The problems in open communication of both ideas and feelings are discussed on page 118 in the section on barriers to open communication. When thinking about the openness of your organization and particularly within the unit you are responsible for, you may find differences in the degree to which people express ideas and feelings.

Your work situation will probably encompass three different audiences for open communication—those above you, your peers, and those who report to you. How willing and able you are to be open will depend not only on the individual involved but on his or her role in the hierarchy. The audiences and topics for open communication are summarized in the Table below. Use the following scale to determine how open you are with each audience and topic:

1 = not at all open; 2 = seldom open; 3 = open depending on situation; 4 = usually open; 5 = very open.

	Listening		*Telling*	
	Ideas	*Feelings*	*Ideas*	*Feelings*
Those above you	_____	_____	_____	_____
Peers	_____	_____	_____	_____
Those who report to you	_____	_____	_____	_____

Open communication is not the *indiscriminate* dissemination of information or expression of feelings, which would be as dysfunctional as withholding information and avoiding feelings. Organizations sometimes "solve" communication problems by sending out more information, but the communication is usually only one way. This does not necessarily assure that more understanding has occurred, only that the number of meetings and pounds of memos have increased. An increase in communication which is not based on an understanding of employees' needs can result in information overload. A balance between disclosure and information overload is needed in the day-to-day business operations.

The mutual sharing of information along with the freedom to ask questions and to disagree has proved quite difficult to achieve in organizations. The arguments for and against the concept (however it may work in practice) are:

Closed	*Open*
People couldn't handle the quantity of information.	People need to be allowed choice in what information they need.
Line workers aren't really interested in anything other than the paycheck.	Some are interested in a lot of things; managers are making the choice for them.
It's too risky to let people know of plans; there will be changes before everything is set.	People are better able to deal with uncertainty than with total ambiguity.
People would get overly emotional if the atmosphere were open.	Feelings are a part of life (even in organizations); to ignore them is to be unrealistic.
The organization would lose control.	If you are knowledgeable, then problems can be prevented.
Management is in the best position to make decisions.	Innovation and responding to change calls for openness and spontaneity.

How important is it to have an environment in which ideas and feelings can be expressed, listened to, accepted, and, as appropriate, acted upon? The following examples should help you to examine the need for open communication.

One plant in another division experiences layoffs, and people in your division are anxious that it may happen to them.

Your industry is subject to intense attack in the press to the point where people resent the press and/or the organization.

The EEO program has resulted in a lot of visibility and promotions for women and minorities, while white men feel bitter over what appears to be special opportunity for others.

Your organization decided not to give a cost of living adjustment in the years of double-digit inflation.

A technician has found serious errors in a major project which has the support of top management.

A clerk with a good performance record is denied a raise because of a poor attendance record due to a long illness.

A task force you are on does not allow open discussion and dissent.

Another organization bought your company, and a number of people have been retired early or asked to leave.

The city agency you work for is not reporting expenditures properly to the federal government.

An intern or nurse observes improper procedures by a staff doctor.

In each of these situations important data exist or strong feelings are evoked which will influence employees' behavior. To overlook the issues *or* the feelings is to deny reality. Yet that is exactly what some organizations do.

BARRIERS TO OPEN COMMUNICATION

The tendency to filter bad news and to exaggerate good news is hardly a phenomenon of modern organizations. In the fifth century B.C., Sophocles commented, "It is the merit of a general to import good news and to conceal the bad." The wisdom of the Greeks has been confirmed by twentieth-century researchers who have found that "officials' perceptions will operate so as to partially screen out data adverse to their own interests, and to magnify those favorable to their interest." [6]

What constitutes "bad news" to you as a manager?

Your top project is two months behind schedule.

The underwriter made an error on a major case.

A key customer was unhappy with the last shipment.

---

[6] Anthony Downs, *Inside Bureaucracy* (Boston: Little, Brown, 1967), p. 118.

The parts you need for a rush order are not available.

Your most productive performer is dissatisfied with the job.

None of these events can be interpreted as good news, but what is the effect of having the information delayed, distorted, or not reported at all? In most cases the effect will be another, larger problem which then becomes a crisis. Common sense tells us that, above all, managers need to hear "bad news." To be able to solve problems, shift resources, or prepare an alternative requires timely, accurate information.

The difficulty in finding out bad news is not just a problem for middle managers, but for chief executives as well. After setting up the Office of Management and Budget, Roy Ash became the chief executive of a troubled company, Addressograph–Multigraph. In reviewing their research and development program, Ash found that "one of his hardest jobs was getting information from the managers of A–M's Multigraphic Division. . . .'Enough people were emotionally involved and kind of skewed the data, I think unconsciously,' he says. 'When you've fathered something, it's hard to admit that you've got a mongoloid.' "[7] After Ash's probing, it became apparent that a key project with a $10 million investment had to be scrapped.

There are six built-in factors which make it difficult to achieve open communication: organizational roles, fear of emotionality, evaluation, investment in maintaining the relationship, loss of control, and organizational constraints. Knowledge of these barriers can help you to plan and develop the practices which will encourage open communication.

Organizational Roles

Organizations, with their hierarchies and position descriptions, define roles which are then fulfilled by individuals. The amount of power associated with the position is usually indicated: chief executive, vice president, director, manager, department head, supervisor. The roles and the corresponding power carry with them expectations of how the individual in that position should behave. And the organization provides symbols for the role, such as a title, the location of the office, the type of furniture, and includes some element of deference in the communication pattern. People find out about these deferences through the informal system; who initiates the contact, how much information is to be shared, who asks the questions, which person talks the most. For ex-

[7] Louis Kraar, "Roy Ash is Having Fun at Addressogrief-Multigrief," *Fortune*, February 17, 1978, p. 49.

ample, as a supervisor in a government agency, your role would probably not call for you to initiate conversations with the commissioner of the agency. How people in your organization perceive your role and the power it carries with it has a large measure of influence on their ability and willingness to be open with you.

Whatever your work experience or level in the organization, your immediate supervisor or boss is what psychologist Sidney Jourard terms a "significant other." He or she occupies an important place in your life, having the power to change your job assignment, give financial reward, recommend or approve promotions. This degree of power, indeed, makes the person significant to you. And you are that "significant other" in the organization to the people who report to you.

Organizational roles, with their prescribed patterns of behaviors, can be quite unhealthy because they often limit what can be said to whom and under what circumstances. Jourard found that healthy people were able to disclose themselves to others who were significant to them, but with risk. "There is probably no experience more terrifying than disclosing oneself to 'significant others' whose probable reactions are assumed, but not known." [8] It is only through disclosure that we can get feedback, be confirmed as an individual, and at the same time get the information to monitor and perhaps alter our behavior.

Fear of Feelings

Sharing feelings involves a higher risk because it makes one vulnerable and may place a heavier investment in the relationship than you are willing to make. Knowing how another feels supplies you with personal, indeed, sometimes intimate, information. Being aware of someone's distress or joy can be a bond which may be discomforting. When the feelings are related to organizational matters, the risk increases. Expressing feelings, especially negative ones, about decisions in the organization is not usually accepted.

Organizational norms operate to preclude feelings as legitimate topics. Seldom explicitly stated, the norm goes something like, "Feelings have no place in business. We have to deal only with the facts." Unfortunately such a norm denies the complexity of human behavior and cuts us off from an important aspect of being human. Argyris interpreted executive behavior he observed as adhering to a value system which discouraged open expression or acceptance of feelings. [9]

[8] Sidney Jourard, *The Transparent Self* (Princeton: Van Nostrand Reinhold, 1971), p. 31.
[9] Chris Argyris, "Interpersonal Barriers to Decision-Making," *Harvard Business Review*, March-April, 1966, p. 85.

The difficulty lies in not distinguishing *having* feelings (being angry over not being promoted), *expressing* feelings (I resent not getting this promotion), and *acting* on those feelings (taking a day off, crying, or screaming in rage and breaking the furniture). The fear of actions which could be labeled emotional has probably operated to try to close off feelings altogether. To be sure, managers will be uncomfortable with extreme behavior and most often it is not appropriate in a work setting. The anxiety over the extreme leads to a dysfunctional behavior, acting "as if" prople don't have feelings and assuming there is no middle ground. Carrying out this pretense is costly not only to the individual, but to the organization as well.

Evaluation

If it appears that openness will result in a negative evaluation, then the odds are against the disclosure. A person who thinks that a disclosure will result in a judgment—being a complainer, being unable to take the pressure—will have difficulty being open with you.

Some people have difficulty receiving a negative response because it is taken as an evaluation of their total person. It is somewhat arbitrary to separate criticism of ideas and of the person, but both listener and teller need to make the effort. This ability to separate criticism of ideas and the person is greatly helped when the sender uses descriptive language. Often the way in which the comment is phrased does make it a personal attack. People who have bad experiences as a result of being open will find it difficult to overcome that history. They "hear" devaluation of themselves as individuals. In an open environment people are able to hear and separate negative information which has to do with ideas and that which has to do with them as individuals.

Investment in Maintaining the Relationship

It is natural to prefer satisfying relationships and to want to maintain them. The fear that disclosure will disrupt the relationship reduces our ability to be open. Some people fear total disruption, i.e., being fired. The nature and purpose of the relationship between two people is an important determinant of self-disclosure. If we are uncertain or anxious about the response of the other person, we may not risk the disclosure. The desire (and organizational need) to maintain the relationship often lowers the degree of freedom to share information and feelings. This seems a high price to pay in any relationship. Without mutual sharing, problems go unsolved; we are deprived of knowing how our actions impact others and denied the opportunity to exercise any influence.

The irony is that people need openness in relationships that really matter. In our desire to maintain a relationship, we may assume that the other person will not be able to tolerate negative information. In some cases that is probably true, but the assumption goes untested more often than not. In organizations there are important relationships in which people do not know how other people will respond to feelings, bad news, or a question. This lack of knowledge about the response, and the assumption that the relationship cannot tolerate openness, are responsible for a great deal of closed communication.

Loss of Control

All of us have had the experience of sharing information or feelings which came back to haunt us. The potential loss of control over the information and its consequences hinders disclosure. Uncertainty over what will be done with the information, if it will be held against us at some future date, is a significant barrier to open communication. An executive in a consulting firm once was asked suddenly by his superior to "fantasize" out loud (at a management committee meeting) about what he would like to see changed in his job responsibilities. Several months later, part of the disclosure was used by the superior to "justify" a reorganization that adversely affected the executive, who felt manipulated and "sandbagged."

Sometimes we assume that people will not be able to accept negative or ambiguous information, and therefore decide not to disclose it. Withholding information can be based on anxiety over loss of control: "If people really knew what was going on. . . ." Managers have a lot of fantasies as to how that sentence can be completed. Yet, without information, freedom is reduced and you have to work very hard to maintain control. Figure 6.1a demonstrates the cycle of communication assumptions and loss of control. Figure 6.1b shows how different assumptions can bring about very different results.

Not sharing problems with those who work for you means they never have the opportunity to contribute to solutions. Having never tried to disagree with the boss only confirms the assumption that you are not free to disagree. During the course of a day, you will make many decisions whether or not to be open, with someone above you, with your peers, or with someone who reports to you. Closely examining your assumptions is one means to begin developing open communi-

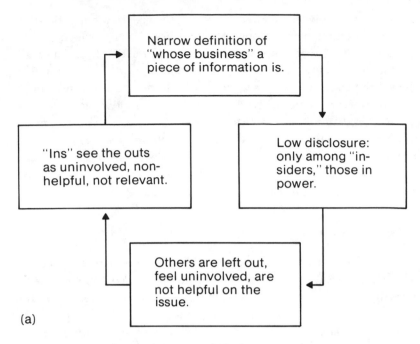

Figure 6.1 Circularity of the control/disclosure process. (After Fritz Steele, *The Open Organization: The Impact of Secrecy and Disclosure on People and Organizations,* © 1975, Addison-Wesley, Reading, MA, p. 117. Reprinted with permission.)

cation. The issue is how to determine the limits of openness and recognize feelings, and at the same time assure the quality and accuracy of information.

One of the factors which you must overcome in developing open communication is the tendency for people to govern their communication behavior in light of what appears to be their best interests.[10] The manager's job, then, is to assure that open communication is in the *employee's* best interests.

Organizational Restrictions

Openness is not an all-or-nothing concept. Two primary conditions restrict openness at the organizational level: (1) that which would result in a competitive disadvantage, and (2) that which would reveal confidential facts about an employee. Even within these restrictions some

[10] Redding, op. cit., p. 392.

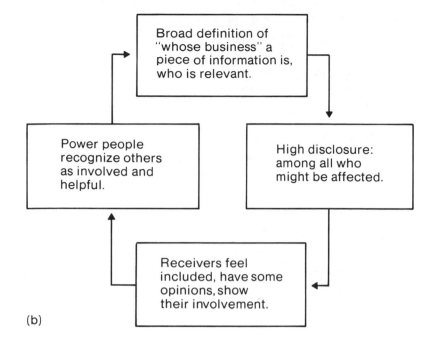

(b)

organizations have faced up to the need for wider disclosure and found ways to safeguard privacy.

These restrictions pertain primarily to external communication, that with stock holders, consumer groups, the press, regulatory agencies, and those institutions which may seek employee information. The line between internal communication (with employees) and external communication (with various sectors of the public) is increasingly blurred. More and more, the policies and practices which guide external and internal communication need to be consistent with those which guide internal communication.

Competitive Disadvantage   BankAmerica, which operates in a highly regulated industry, saw the need to change their disclosure policies and procedures in 1976. After months of study, they developed a voluntary disclosure code which encourages open communication. The code specifies the principles of disclosure and categories of information treated by the code. The task force identified the constraints the bank faced:

1. Disclosure must not violate the privacy rights of individuals or institutions.
2. The corporation cannot disclose information that, if published, might impair its own effectiveness.

3. The corporation cannot disclose speculative or judgmental material that might induce unwarranted effects.
4. To avoid inviting misinterpretation, BankAmerica insists on presentation of factual material in a manner that best promotes real understanding, correct interpretation, and accurate comparison.
5. To avoid adding unduly to information gathering and dissemination, BankAmerica will disclose only data whose usefulness, in contributing to an understanding of the company's activities, justifies the expense of providing it. Preparation of special costly studies will be discouraged or made subject to a charge.

The president, A. W. Clausen, in the preamble to the code, stated the principle as one of accessibility. "The machinery for disclosure will be there, and in most cases the rule of thumb will be: 'Ask and you shall receive.' But there can be no guarantee of instant availability, and no breach of the constraints on releasing confidential customer, employee, proprietary and speculative information." [11]

Even with these very real constraints, the code describes an environment in which disclosure objectives can be met.

1. To provide the men and women who manage BankAmerica with a continuing guide keeps effective disclosure a principal objective of corporate policy.
2. To facilitate disclosure of information that has been determined, not by the corporation but by its constituencies, to be useful and relevant in understanding and evaluating Bank America's activities.
3. To encourage disclosure of information in ways which can be easily understood by all concerned.
4. To give the public ready access, to the extent permitted by law, to information the corporation currently provides in its routine reporting to regulatory agencies.
5. To define the limits of voluntary disclosure—that is, to respond to the public's question, "Why not?"

Clearly BankAmerica is seeking to assist its managers in responding to the mass of data the organization produces and those who are interested in that information. They have answered hundreds of requests for information, many of them on Equal Employment Opportunity and the Affirmative Action programs. Other requests have dealt with

---

[11] BankAmerica Disclosure Code, 1977, pp. 3–6.

conflict of interest, vendors, organization charts, and proxy procedures. BankAmerica still stands as the first bank in the list of the Fortune Fifty. Disclosure has not had the dire consequences that some people feared it would bring. Although the code pertains primarily to outside constituencies—consumer groups, shareholders—employees may also avail themselves of this process.

Privacy

The second restriction on organizational openness is the need to protect employee privacy. Professor of public law and government, Alan F. Westin, has pointed out that there are "well documented concerns of employees and executives over the confidentiality of personnel information maintained by their employers, especially in the new computerized data systems widely used for personnel work."[12] A few states have passed laws governing personnel records and the United States Privacy Protection Study Commission Report have given impetus to laws for the protection of information.

H.R. 285, known as the Comprehensive Right to Privacy Act, is currently before the House of Representatives.[13] The Privacy Act outlines ten key principles for information practice. Five of these principles are critical to employee record keeping.

1. There should be no personal information system whose existence is secret.
2. Individuals must be able to find out what information is in a record and how it is used.
3. Information should not be used unless it is accurate and current.
4. There should be procedures for the individual to correct, erase, or amend inaccurate, obsolete, or irrelevant information.
5. There should be a clearly prescribed procedure for an individual to prevent personal information collected for one purpose from being used for another purpose without his consent.[14]

Although the proposed legislation does not include employee records, privacy is of concern to business. The adoption of voluntary codes is being advocated. Cummins Engine, Equitable Life Assurance Society, Connecticut-General Life Insurance are among the companies which have already adopted such codes.

---

[12] Alan F. Westin, "A New Move Toward Employee Rights," *New York Times*, April 23, 1978.
[13] Before the House of Representatives as of Spring, 1979.
[14] H. R. 285 introduced to the 95th Congress by Mr. Conte, January 4, 1977, pp. 2–3.

IBM, because of the nature of its business and strong views on the rights of employees, has taken the lead in supporting a voluntary approach to employee privacy. In testimony submitted to the Senate, IBM stated that employee surveys have shown that their voluntary code announced in 1975 is working. Further, "IBM strongly supports voluntary action on the part of industry in lieu of legislation and additional regulation."[15]

Their procedures describe, "What information it is permissible to ask a job applicant for, what information goes where, who can use it, what is available to line managers versus what is available only to medical people."[16] They found that information was sought from job applicants that wasn't really needed and that hearsay was recorded in personnel files. Managers are now held responsible for seeing to it that only job-related information is kept in the files.

Job-related information—performance appraisals, performance plans, records of awards, and sales records—is available to the employee and to managers who are making decisions regarding that employee. Importantly, employees can ask for a correction in their records. IBM has found that the performance appraisal is a key document in the personnel file.

Privacy procedures can be complex, detailing who gets to see what information under what circumstances. With technology capable of storing millions of bits of data, the validity and use of that information needs to be safeguarded. Organizations accumulate a great deal of data about their employees, and protecting the privacy of that data is an important element in open communication. Earlier in this chapter, loss of control and evaluation were discussed as barriers to open communication. When people know that only relevant information is recorded, that access is clearly delineated, and that the right to verify the information exists, then ambiguity and anxiety over disclosure are reduced. An atmosphere of appropriate safeguards can only enhance open communication.

EFFECTS OF CLOSED COMMUNICATION

There are examples of organizations which have either ignored or punished those who did disclose critical information. This behavior results

---

[15] "Informational Privacy, Employment and Personnel Record-Keeping,: Submission to the Senate Judiciary Subcommittee on the Constitution," International Business Machine Corporation, Armonk, NY, October 17, 1978, p. 16.
[16] IBM's Guidelines to Employee Privacy," an interview with Frank T. Cary, *Harvard Business Review*, September-October, 1976, p. 84.

in the suppression of errors and allows problems to become crises which then call for drastic action or result in damage to the organization.

In the late 1960s Goodrich engineers developed a four-disc brake system for a military aircraft. A junior engineer did not think that design would meet specifications, and tests bore him out. Apparently, data were fudged, and the "good" news of the system's success was passed up the line. A congressional investigation indicated that Goodrich's top-level management had not known what was going on in the plant.[17]

Richardson–Merrill was developing a drug, MER 29, to repress cholesterol. The lab tests were not very supportive of the drug. A lab technician, asked to falsify records, protested, but was told to do what the executive had ordered. Compensation damages of over $100,000 were paid to a man who developed severe side effects from taking the drug, and the company paid an $80,000 fine for making false statements to the FDA, when it pleaded no contest to the charge.[18]

More recently the Equity Funding scandal shook the insurance industry. This organization's subsidiary Equity Funding Life Insurance wrote and "sold" policies to bogus people and then sold these policies to other companies. This is not a case of one technician or engineer who could not get heard, but of teams of people who worked to cover up the operation. "Keeping the auditors, stockholders, purchasers of policies and others in the dark required—and got—the cooperation of the entire organization."[19]

These examples demonstrate what happens when "bad news" is not accepted. The brake system did not meet government specifications, the drug did cause damage and was pulled off the market, and Equity Funding collapsed. Although the senior management at Goodrich were not aware of the falsified reports, there were individual managers who did know. At Equity Funding, many employees and managers knew. You may have examples from your own work experience where problems were known but not communicated upward or, if known, were not acknowledged. Later the organization paid a price for this behavior.

In addition, "closed communication" cuts you off from your employees, their questions, their concerns, their problems, and their complaints. You may not be able to deal with all of them immediately, but it is important to know what is on your employees' minds. More than one organization has been surprised when an attitude survey showed

---

[17] Christopher D. Stone, *Where the Law Ends: The Social Control of Corporate Behavior*, (New York: Harper & Row 1976), pp. 165–166.
[18] Stone, *Where the Law Ends*, pp. 54–56.
[19] *Ibid.*, p. 68.

that people felt their managers did not listen to them or appear concerned with their problems.

Upward communication programs are one way of tackling this issue, but are intended for those problems which cannot be effectively handled within the line of management. Often, by the time an employee gets to the upward communication program, the concern has become intensified and is more difficult to resolve. Open communication, as described in this chapter, cannot overcome all employee concerns, but it will go a long way in reducing the frequency and intensity of complaints. Employee relations issues are best solved at the point where they occur—between the employee and immediate supervisor.

BUILDING OPEN COMMUNICATION

Now that you know what is working against you, you can examine ways to overcome the barriers to open communication. First, consider the true extent of your own desire for openness. Open communication is a daily way of working, not a gimmick or a fad. What is the payoff for you?

Benefits

Knowledge of work and technical problems as they arise

Fewer crises

Greater ability to solve problems

More freedom for yourself and others to make choices about matters which affect the individual

Increased awareness of how people feel about their jobs and the organization

Greater capacity to develop staff

An environment which allows people to be human, rather than fulfilling roles

More likely innovation

Increased capacity to respond to change

These benefits are laden with values about people, work, and organizations. You need to be clear about your values before endeavoring to build open communication. Thoughtfully examine the degree to which you agree with the following values:

1. It is better to know negative information than not to know.

2. Information helps solve problems.
3. Feelings are an important aspect of human behavior at work.
4. People ought to have a voice in matters which affect them at work.
5. Roles, if taken to the extreme, are dysfunctional.

If you do not agree, in general, with these values, open communication is not for you. Efforts to give employees a "sense" of open communication, rather than the real thing, will ultimately fail. On the other hand, if these statements are congruent with your own values, you will find it easier to work at open communication.

Employee Needs

The second step in building open communication is to understand employee needs. Employees' desire for more information is supported by extensive research. Topics which rank highest in need for receiving information are:

How organization decisions are made that affect my job

Promotion and advancement opportunities
How job-related problems are handled
How I am being judged
Pay and benefits
Organizational policies

Employees want to *send* information on the following topics:

Evaluation of performance of superiors
Complaints about job and working conditions
Reports of job activity and progress
Requests for information needed to do my job
Requests for clarification of confusing work instructions [20]

These data were gathered from employees in a variety of organizations like banking, manufacturing, hospitals, schools, and government agencies. No matter what type of business or nonprofit organization you are in, it's likely that people want to both receive and send more information. In short more openness is needed.

As an individual manager, you may not be in a position to influ-

---

[20] Gerald M. Goldhaber, Michael P. Yates, D. Thomas Porter, and Richard Lesniak, "State of the Art, Organizational Communication: 1978," *Human Communication Research*, Fall, 1978, p. 82.

ence communication on organization decisions, pay and benefits, and organizational policies. These are most often handled by corporate communications and/or personnel. The matters of most concern are those affecting performance and progress, job activity, and work instructions. It is in these areas where you exercise direct control, and where open communication can be most effective.

Opportunities

In order for mutuality in sharing of information and feelings to develop, communication opportunities need to be provided. The opportunities can be made available in different ways, such as meetings, performance appraisals, walks through the work area, and creating special opportunities.

Meetings   In Chapter 5, the various purposes for meetings were discussed. It would be facile to say that all groups must have regular staff meetings. In general this is true, but there must be a clear purpose for meeting. Open communication is a way of behaving, not just a reason for getting people together. At meetings, check the following indicators of openness:

1. People ask each other questions as well as the manager.
2. Differences of opinion are expressed.
3. Most people contribute something to the meeting.
4. Evaluation and criticism are directed toward ideas, not individuals.
5. People recognize and accept the interests of others.
6. Feelings are acknowledged and accepted.

In addition to staff meetings, meetings need to be held when changes are pending or ambiguity exists—at times of reorganization, merger, major policy change, or uncertain financial results. Not having meetings under these circumstances will only contribute to uncertainty and anxiety. Part of human nature is a desire to reduce uncertainity, and people will be seeking information from whatever sources they can find. Rather than risk inaccurate, distorted, or fragmented information, it is better to tell what you do know as well as identify what you don't know. Acknowledging lack of information is vital to maintaining credibility.

Performance Appraisal   This important opportunity to build openness between two individuals has been reviewed in depth in Chapter 4.

Achieving the goals of any performance discussion depends largely on the degree of openness the two people are able to have with each other. Following the guidelines for describing behavior, listening, responding to feelings, and asking questions are the keys to openness and mutuality in this situation. At the same time the restraints to communication need to be remembered. In a performance review you are in an evaluative situation where your role and power are quite clear. Extra attention is needed to separate the description of performance from the judgment.

Walk Through the Work Area   In many organizations with which I am familiar, both professional and clerical staffs complain that they rarely see the manager. This comment pertains not only to their immediate supervisor, but also to the senior managers. Your responsibilities may often call for you to be away from the work area, or in your office with the door closed.

Even with these pressures, try and find time to chat informally with people, to be visible and accessible. These walks should not be seen as spying or as a means to short-circuit the supervisors who report to you. The simple fact is that it is difficult to ask questions or discuss problems with someone you barely know. Make it a practice to get to know people on an informal, face-to-face basis. Use the time to find out about the work and the environment in which people spend one-third of their day.

Creating Your Own Opportunity   In some circumstances a formal or even informal opportunity may not present itself when needed. Or, if available, the occasion may not be appropriate for the matter you wish to discuss. Taking responsibility for your own behavior requires at times that you create the opportunity for discussion.

If a problem is plaguing you, taking a lot of time and energy, identify the person you need to talk to. Request an appointment, drop by his or her office, write a memo, do whatever is needed within limits of appropriateness in your organization. You may need to violate some of the norms of communication (not a good thing if a regular practice), but some circumstances call for it.

Analyze the Risks of Disclosure

Determining the risks of disclosure is not a one-time event; rather, the decision is made repeatedly. Believing in open communication does not mean you automatically share information. The circumstances will have to be examined each time you are faced with such a decision. At times it may be to your detriment to either share information or listen to reports of problems, and your own boss may not always agree with you. If you believe that people have a right to be heard and to know about matters which affect their careers, you need to be equipped to assess potential disclosure situations. The model in Table 6.1 shows conditions of both low and high disclosure and the short-term and long-term effects of each disclosure decision. In each of the circumstances listed below, weigh the risks and the outcomes of disclosure.

TABLE 6.1   Disclosure-Risk Model

	Short-Term Effects	*Long-Term Effects*
Low Disclosure	Maintain comfort	Issues avoided/not solved
	Gain social approval	Maintain stable relationship
	Avoid embarrassment	
	Lose opportunity to speak directly	Loss of credibility if issues become obvious
	Low cost/save time	Don't learn from the past
High Disclosure	Confront immediate concerns	Issues dealt with
	Share part of self	Takes more time
	Some discomfort	More learning possible
	Some embarrassment	Adapt to changing situation
	Possible disapproval from those who don't approve of disclosure	Greater credibility
	Cost of communication	Need for communication budget and staff

SOURCE: Developed from material discussed by Fritz Steele in *The Open Organization.*

Should you describe the high-pressure environment of your work to the job applicant?

Do you tell the department VP that the budget cuts will have serious consequences on customer service in the long run?

Should you object when someone you find it hard to work with is assigned to your task force?

Do you tell your boss of project delays or wait in the hopes you can overcome them?

Do you tell the people who report to you that a reorganization is pending even though the specific changes have not yet been decided?

Should you ask your boss about your potential next career steps?

Taking the last example for the list of disclosure decisions, Table 6.2 shows how the model works in practice.

TABLE 6.2   Application of Risk-Disclosure Model

	Short-Term Effects	*Long-Term Effects*
Low Disclosure	Maintain comfort level with the boss	Concerns over your future are unresolved, less in your control
	Not be embarrassed by manager not knowing	
	Save time in discussing your career	Stability of relationship is maintained
	Lose opportunity to get direct information on your future	May get resentful toward boss and the organization
	Don't risk his disapproval for raising the issue	Have no opportunity to learn from current experience what might be helpful on future positions
High Disclosure	Deal immediately with your concern over career in the organization	Find out if he or she knows/ has a plan you can discuss/ can find out for you
	May be uncomfortable or embarrassed temporarily	Could learn what you need to do to get ready for the next position
High Disclosure	He or she could disapprove of you for raising the issue	Increase credibility between you and your boss, knowing where each stands on the issue

The decision to disclose concern over your career is an individual one and must be based on an assessment of the total situation. The model provides a way to systematically examine the long-term effects and weigh them carefully against short-term effects. Overall, lack of information reduces freedom. If you do not know what the available career choices are, what the organization's plans are, if in turn they are not aware of your interests, desires, and plans, then the career alternatives are reduced for both of you. The only way to act freely is to share information and make choices.

The short-term gains for low disclosure will warrant withholding or being less than open at times. If, however, the long-term costs were considered, different decisions might be made in many organizations.

Check the Perception of Your Openness

"My door is always open. My people can come in here any time they want and speak what's on their mind." How many times have you heard that statement and said to yourself, "Who is this person kidding? Go in there at your own risk."

My own experience and that of researchers who have studied openness supports the contention that managers greatly overestimate the perceptions others hold of their openness. You may have every desire to maintain an "Open Door Policy," but you may not have recognized the barriers which exist within the organization and for the individual. Or you may, unknowingly, criticize people who come in with problems and questions. People are more willing to be open when they think that the manager is willing to listen to employees' ideas and complaints. How you respond to questions, challenges, and expressions of concerns will markedly influence the perception of your openness. You may not always agree or be able to solve the particular difficulty. Being an active, empathic listener, asking good questions, and doing follow-up are more important than proclaiming, "My door is always open."

Think about the following symptoms which indicate you may not be open to others.

1. I am surprised to find out about problems.
2. People transfer or quit this unit because they are dissatisfied.
3. I am called on fairly frequently to "fight fires."
4. People generally agree with my decisions.
5. We frequently spend time redoing work.
6. I am caught short without alternatives when things go wrong.
7. This is not a pleasant place to be.
8. I don't need information from others to make decisions.

No one of these items, taken singly, is a sign of closed communication. Many reasons could be found for people agreeing with your decisions, including the fact that you make good ones! If, however, several of these symptoms are present, your perception of how open you are may not be accurate, and some effort at open communication is needed.

There are several ways to check out the validity of your view of how open the climate is. Many organizations regularly undertake attitude surveys which could provide some communication data. The results would have to be available to you on a unit basis in order for the information to be specific enough for you to interpret. Attitude surveys are seldom very specific on communication, as their goal is to sample the total climate. Your Training and Development or Organization Development department, or an outside consultant, could help you to gather information from your employees.

One survey, developed by Harry Dennis,[21] which specifically addresses communication climate, is included in the Appendixes. An adaptation of his survey which can be used to evaluate your own capacity for open communication appears at the end of this chapter.

Be careful of administering such questionnaires to others on your own. Data of this kind should be gathered and analyzed by a neutral third party. People need to be comfortable with how the information will be used and who will know the source of any particular response. Many employees would freely express their views while others may be unsure of the risks and thus opt for low disclosure. If you work with a third party, it is especially important that you listen nondefensively to the results and be willing to commit to change as issues are identified.

SUMMARY

Of the 87.3 million people employed in the civilian workforce, only one in ten is self-employed. Most people who work do so with and for others; many of the self-employed have people working for them. A significant number of workers fall under the aegis of mammoth organizations. The Fortune 500 industrial companies alone account for 15.8 million employees. Within this context, individuals need to find a means to have some measure of influence on their work lives and to be treated as mature adults.

At the same time organizations need to increase their capacity to provide information and attempt to share meaning with employees. Managers ought to be able to listen to the experiences of people who work for them, and at least acknowledge that people function with

---

[21] Harry S. Dennis, "A Theoretical and Empirical Study of Managerial Climate in Complex Organizations," doctoral dissertation, Purdue University, 1974.

both reason and feelings. "Upward" and "downward" communication do not appear to be effective responses as they ignore a central fact about the communication process: Communication is an interactive person process based on individual perception. The manager who is able to maintain open communication will probably not be able to fully understand each employee. Yet such a manager will be able to understand enough of the time to maintain an effective unit for the individuals.

TRW, which employs over 93,000 people, has a sophisticated program of employee communication. They developed communication principles and guidelines which place primary responsibility on managers:

> Communications to and from each employee and the immediate supervisor is particularly important and is the most crucial communications link in developing an ongoing, open system of listening, talking and acting that affects attitudes and productivity.[22]

This statement by a highly successful organization succinctly describes the manager's communication responsibilities in all organizations. This chapter is intended to help you carry out those responsibilities.

---

[22] "Employee Communications Principles and Guidelines," TRW, Cleveland, Ohio.

SELF-ASSESSMENT OF BUILDING OPEN COMMUNICATION

Check the extent to which you do each of the following:

	Very Little	Little	Some	Great	Very Great
1. I help others feel free to talk with me.	___	___	___	___	___
2. I understand my employees' job problems.	___	___	___	___	___
3. I encourage others to let me know when things are going wrong on the job.	___	___	___	___	___
4. I make it easy for others to do their best work.	___	___	___	___	___
5. I express confidence in my employees' ability to perform their job.	___	___	___	___	___
6. I encourage others to bring new information to my attention, even when that new information may be bad news.	___	___	___	___	___
7. Others feel that the things they tell me are usually important.	___	___	___	___	___
8. I am willing to tolerate argument and to give a fair hearing to all points of view.	___	___	___	___	___
9. I listen to the people who report to me when they state things that are bothering them.	___	___	___	___	___
10. It's safe for my people to say what they are really thinking.	___	___	___	___	___

SELF-ASSESSMENT OF BUILDING OPEN COMMUNICATION (Continued)

Check the extent to which you do each of the following:

	Very Little	Little	Some	Great	Very Great
11. People who report to me are frank and candid with me.					
12. My people can "sound off" about job frustrations to me.					
13. My people can tell me about how they feel I am managing the work group.					
14. My people are able to disagree with me.					
15. People can communicate "bad news" to me without fear of retaliation on my part.					
16. I believe I really understand the people who report to me.					
17. My people think that they understand me.					
18. The information I receive from my subordinates is reliable.					

SOURCE: Adapted from Harry Dennis' Communication Climate Inventory.

CHAPTER 7
DEVELOPING A PERSONAL
COMMUNICATION PLAN

The readers of this book want to be more effective managers, to be more competent handling the "people responsibilities" inherent in the manager's job, to be more productive, to be of more value to the organization, to be more satisfied with relationships at work. You may be studying communication on your own, in a management development program, or in a college classroom. In any case the ultimate goal is to improve communication and managerial effectiveness. Achievement of this goal will entail some behavior change.

Communication is a complex set of behaviors which you have been learning throughout your entire life. Some of the patterns are old and will be difficult to change. In addition to the burden of old patterns is the elusive nature of communication in modern organizations: "We have more attempts at communication today, that is, more attempts to talk to others, and a surfeit of communication media. . . . Yet communications has proven as elusive as the Unicorn." [1]

The Unicorn is a mythical animal, but communication skills are not myths. They are as real and as complex as the people and the organizations in which communication takes place. My own experience and that of managers I have worked with clearly demonstrate that behavior change, or at least, modification, is entirely possible—not easy, only possible.

The preceding chapters discussed the functions, concepts, and skills

---

[1] Peter Drucker, *Management: Tasks, Responsibilities, Practices* (New York: Harper & Row, 1973), p. 482.

for effective communication. This chapter outlines a process for behavior change which can keep this from being just another book on management. Developing a personal communication plan calls for you to work through the following phases:

Assess current level of effectiveness.
State change goals.
Identify knowledge and skills required.
Analyze benefits.
Determine the appropriate situation for new behavior.
Identify obstacles in your way and means to overcome them.
Monitor and evaluate your progress.

As you complete each phase, write out your plan using the forms at the end of the chapter.

ASSESS SKILL EFFECTIVENESS

Each of the chapters covers a specific management activity. Although the communication concepts and skills can apply to more than one activity, the analysis of message types (Chapter 1) and communication fits together like this:

Regulative: Explain the policies and procedures which regulate the organization.
Task: Get work done at meetings. There is more to accomplishing your tasks than meetings, but for managers, this is an increasingly important way of getting the work done.
Innovative: Building open communication is the key to identifying and solving problems as well as gathering new ideas.
Integrative: Performance appraisal is the pivotal process which enables people to understand their role in the organization and to feel valued as individuals.

With this framework in mind, assess your skill effectiveness. Self-awareness and feedback are two essential components of this process. Self-awareness is knowledge which can lead to insight into yourself. When we experience such insight, familiar events are reorganized in such a way that new solutions to problems become available.[2] The self-assessment forms are intended to increase awareness of your behavior and

---

[2] Rosalea A. Schonbar, "Interpretation and Insight in Psychotherapy," in *Use of Interpretation in Treatment,* Emanuel F. Hammer, ed. (New York: Grune & Stratton, 1968), p. 75.

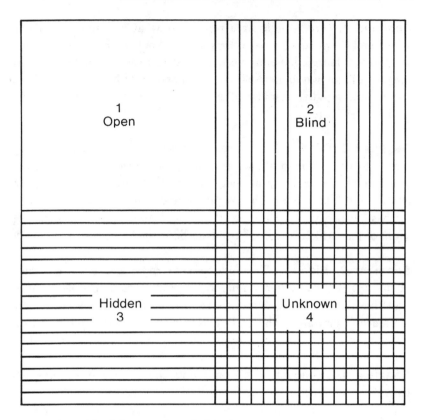

Figure 7.1   The Johari window. (After *Group Processes: An Introduction to Group Dynamics* by Joseph Luft, by permission of Mayfield Publishing Co., copyright © 1963, 1970 Joseph Luft.)

contribute to self-insight. With self-insight, you can reorganize your thinking about communication and approach problems differently.

Feedback, the process of finding out how others perceive you, describes the impact of your behavior on others. Self-perception is not necessarily accurate, so additional information is needed to expand what you know about yourself. You have not only to know what you think you are doing, but to hear and see yourself as others do.

Model for Increasing Self-Awareness

The Johari window shown in Figure 7.1 visually demonstrates the role of self-understanding and feedback as a prerequisite to change.[3] It contains four segments—open, blind, hidden, and unknown—which correspond to the degree of knowledge we have about ourselves.

_____

[3] Joseph Luft, *Group Processes: An Introduction to Group Dynamics* (New York: National Press Books, 1970), p. 11.

Segment 1, Open   This area represents what we know about ourselves and, in general, what others know about us. For example, you are 5 feet 9 inches, have brown eyes, and like to wear vests. Less visible, but still known to yourself and to others, could be the fact that you speak quite rapidly. You and others are aware of this behavior, so it is in the "open" area.

Segment 2, Blind   This segment depicts behavior which is not apparent to you but is to others. You may not realize, for example, that you interrupt frequently at meetings, or that your explanations are confusing to the listener. The people around you know, but the behavior has escaped your awareness. If you wish to change your behavior, some of that which is "blind" needs to be moved into the open area.

Segment 3, Hidden   The hidden area represents what we know about ourselves that others do not know. For example, people often report that they are quite nervous when giving a public speech, but the audience is unaware of this feeling as it is not demonstrated in any observable behavior. The nervousness, then, is in the "hidden" area.

Segment 4, Unknown   This represents an area which is assumed to exist. One could describe it as being in the realm of the unconscious or, more simply, aspects about ourselves which we and others do not know exist. At times, perceptions and feelings from the "unknown" influence behavior. You may have surprised yourself by listening especially well to the problem of a peer, as in the past you did not behave this way. Perhaps something which was "unknown" moved into the blind or open area.

Principles of Behavior Change

From the Johari window Luft derives several principles of behavior change needed to develop a personal communication plan.

1. "The smaller the first quadrant (open), the poorer the communication. That is, if you allow little of yourself to come through to others, communication is unlikely to be effective."
2. "It takes energy to hide, deny, or be blind to behavior which is involved in interaction. When the open area is increased, more of the resources and skills of the individual can be applied to the task."[4]

---

[4] *Ibid.*, p. 15.

It takes energy to ignore your behavior and its effect on others. This energy is better used when you can bring behavior from the blind area into the open area. The Johari window is a model for understanding the role of feedback, adding to the information you have about yourself, and freeing energy to follow through with your plan.

Guidelines for Feedback

The exercises and self-assessment forms should help you to describe the open segment and to discover some of the behaviors in the blind and hidden segments. To check your perceptions and discover some behaviors in the other segments, you need to get some feedback. This can be a difficult task, especially if you are not in a classroom or training environment. Giving and getting feedback is easier in a structured situation with a skilled instructor. Whether in a classroom or on your own, you can use some of these guidelines for getting feedback.

1. Actively seek feedback on areas of communication which are important to you. Let others know that you want feedback on your communication.
2. The person giving the feedback should be able to describe your actual behavior, not evaluate what you should or should not do.
3. The person giving you feedback should be specific rather than general. Telling someone to "communicate better" or to be a "better leader" is too general to be of much use. Specific comments would be, "Your questions usually begin with 'Don't you agree with me that. . . .' so I feel set up." Or, "When people go off on tangents at meetings, you let them wander rather than bringing the group back to the agenda."
4. The feedback should be focused on events which you have both observed and which are fairly current. It should not dwell on the past or on incidents where one or the other was not present. "When we were discussing the new advertising schedule yesterday, you interrupted Susan three times. Then she quit talking altogether." Not, "Three months ago Susan had a hard time at the meeting."
5. Do not allow the person giving the feedback to infer your motives or feelings. Only observable behavior should be included. "You did that because you always want to control the conversation." Instead, "You talked most of the time. I couldn't get a word in."
6. Feedback is most useful when it is well timed, generally at the earliest opportunity after the behavior has occurred. Seek feed-

back when you are "ready" to hear, and have the available time to discuss it.

7. Feedback is a check to assure accuracy of communication. Reflecting what a person has said is a useful way to make sure that you got the message straight. "You're saying, then, that I don't give you enough direction on new projects."

From this list of guidelines, you can see that feedback follows the principles of descriptive rather than inferential language. Do not try and get feedback from a person who does not know how to be descriptive. It will be of little value to you and will only generate defensiveness. The forms at the end of the various chapters could be useful in soliciting feedback from others as they provide concrete descriptions of communication behaviors. Have them filled out only when you trust

TABLE 7.1   Communication Styles by Audience and Situation

		Blaming	Telling	Selling	Problem Solving
Giving Explanations	Those who report to you	___	___	___	___
	Those above you	___	___	___	___
	Peers	___	___	___	___
Performance Appraisal	Those who report to you	___	___	___	___
Meetings	Those who report to you	___	___	___	___
	Those above you	___	___	___	___
	Peers	___	___	___	___
	Mixed groups	___	___	___	___
Building Open Communication	Those who report to you	___	___	___	___
	Those above you	___	___	___	___
	Peers	___	___	___	___
	Totals	___	___	___	___

the other person's ability to observe accurately, respond descriptively, and be empathic to your feelings.

Identify Your Communication Style

Before reviewing the specific skills for each function, determine what your dominant style is from among the four styles described in Chapter 2. Most people find that their style changes depending on the other person and the situation. Yet patterns can be discerned, and one or two styles will emerge as dominant. Use Table 7.1 to analyze your use of each style in different situations. Check only one style for each group in each situation.

Scoring   Scores can range from 0–11. Since most organizations do not have formal performance discussions with peers, there is only one audience for this communication. Often meetings are composed of people from a variety of levels and functions. Consequently there are four scores for the meeting category.

By simply using percentages, you can see how often you use each style. A score of 6 or more (54 percent and above) identifies your dominant style. If you did not score 6 or more on any one style, you have a blend of styles.

Sample Scores	*Percent*	*Number*
Blaming	9	1
Telling	36	4
Selling	54	6
Problem solving	---	

The dominant style in this example is selling; telling is the backup style.

Next examine your style for each group of people with whom you work. The range of scores is 1 to 4 for those who report to you, 1 to 3 for those above you and your peers. Go across the columns and score your style for each group. In Table 7.2, write in the style you use most often with each group. Then indicate whether or not you are satisfied with your communication style for each group.

TABLE 7.2 Communication Style Summary by Audience

	Style	Satisfied	Dissatisfied
With those who report to me	_____	_____	_____
With those above me	_____	_____	_____
With peers	_____	_____	_____

Now that you know your style in different situations, several questions need to be addressed. Do you change styles depending on the situation and the person? If so, why? Changing styles is not necessarily inappropriate if you are reasonably certain you are achieving desired results. You may find that you "tell" those who report to you, "sell" your boss, and "problem solve" with peers. The question is how appropriate and effective are the behaviors? Are you making an assumption that those who report to you always have to be told without giving other styles a chance? Or that your boss always has to be sold without trying telling or problem solving? If you want to change your style in one or more situations, identify the components and behaviors of each by reviewing Chapter 2.

The self-assessment forms from each chapter are repeated on pages 159–169 to make it easier to put together an analysis of your communication. Review each set of skills and identify the specific behaviors you would like to change. Complete planning forms for each function appear at the end of the chapter.

Criteria for Selection of Behavior Change

How can you determine among the array of skills which you want to improve? The criteria listed here are questions to guide your selection.

1. *Are you satisfied with the results you are getting?* In general do people seem to be able to follow through on your explanations, or are there frequent questions, work which has to be redone, policies which are not followed? After performance discussions do you see improvement? Are your meetings an effective use of time and do they produce results in which you are confident? Do people come to you with "bad news"? Are most difficulties and concerns aired openly? Do you go to others with issues which need their attention? Each managerial function has anticipated results, and your communication should be contributing to those results.

2. *How satisfied are you with your own behavior?* Are you comfortable and pleased in most cases when you speak with others? How often do you find yourself regretting the conversation and wishing it could have gone differently? Personal satisfaction is not the only criterion and can be misleading. Often we are comfortable with our behavior only because we are used to it.

3. *How often do others appear to be defensive in response to you?* Communication is essentially an interactive process, one in which each person influences the other. If people often seem closed, unwilling to share information with you, upset in some way, it is likely that you are contributing to their response. We cannot control others' behavior but to some degree responses are "triggered" by the initial communication.

4. *How important is the particular behavior to your organization?* Policies and procedures may play a large or a small part in the functioning of your organization. Meetings may be a way of life to you or take up only a small portion of your time. Perhaps performance appraisal isn't done, but is needed. Your communication climate may already be quite open and not in need of much work on your part. Judge for yourself how important each is to your organization and consequently to your career as you select behaviors for your communication plan.

STATE A CHANGE GOAL

Use the review of skills and criteria above to develop a series of goal statements. A goal should indicate what you want to accomplish. Avoid generalities, as they do not provide enough direction for behavior change.

Weak goal: to improve my explanations
Strong goal: to provide more rationale for changes when explaining procedures to my staff

Weak goal: to be a better leader at meetings
Strong goal: to plan agendas allowing appropriate amounts of time for discussion

Weak goal: to conduct better performance reviews
Strong goal: to write out each employee's performance review and check language for inferential words

Weak goal: to establish a better climate for open communication

Strong goal: to share information about impending changes as quickly as possible

State your goal for each of the four functions.

IDENTIFY KNOWLEDGE AND SKILLS REQUIRED

The goal statements give direction to your plan. Now they need to be translated into specific actions. These actions indicate information or knowledge you need and what behavior is required to carry out the plan. For example:

Goal: to provide more rationale in giving explanations and to ask more questions to assure clarity of issues

Knowledge and skills:

1. Have background information available on key issues.
2. Allow sufficient time.
3. Organize material so it relates to the employees' needs.
4. Identify places in advance where questions could be asked. Determine if open or direct questions are most appropriate.

It may be tempting to do this exercise mentally rather than writing out the goals and knowledge and skills required. Resist that temptation; committing yourself to a written plan is a discipline which forces you to think through the stages of behavior change and to articulate necessary action.

DETERMINE THE APPROPRIATE SITUATION FOR THE NEW BEHAVIOR

No matter how desirable a new behavior may be, it will be difficult to maintain. A reasonably "safe" situation for trial behavior is needed; one which will allow the freedom to take risks, and where there is a reasonable chance of success. Trying new behaviors at random is not likely to provide the kind of practice and reinforcement you need.

Initially it is best to carefully select a situation where you think the odds of a successful trial and positive responses are high. Two meetings are scheduled next week, a staff meeting on problems in the outpatient clinic and a budget session for department heads on cost reduction. Your goal is to help keep the meetings on track and solve problems by asking questions and providing summaries. Knowledge of the individuals, the intensity of the issues, and your own reactions will determine which situation is best for skill development. Here are a few questions to ask as you make your selection:

1. Under what circumstances am I most comfortable personally?
2. Which people are most likely to give me a positive response?
3. When is it likely I will have advance time to prepare?
4. What about the material is likely to make me uncomfortable?
5. Will anybody be present who makes me uncomfortable?

A new behavior, simply because you are not used to it, is likely to make you uncomfortable. Discomfort cannot be eliminated, but it can be reduced by seeking situations where you will receive support from others, have the time to plan, and not be "thrown" by people who are particularly disconcerting. Once you have tried the behavior in a "low-threat" environment, you will be more confident and better able to incorporate the behavior into other, more demanding situations.

DETERMINE THE BENEFITS

Why do you want to change any of your behavior? What is in it for you? For the people who report to you? For the organization? Unless you have benefits clearly in mind, your motivation will flag, and the effort required to make change will be lost in the pressures of other demands and past habits.

Productivity and Service Results

The major thrust of this book is to relate communication to your management responsibilities and the ongoing work. One key source of motivation is the production or service results you want to achieve.

What can you hope to accomplish by holding meetings in the way described in Chapter 4? Meetings which have goals make it easier for others to participate, can result in better decisions, have easier implementation of a plan. For each function, identify the specific results you want to achieve within your work unit.

Development of Others

Managing by the authority of position, using the power of your role, is becoming more and more difficult in modern organizations.[5] The lessening of authority does not necessarily mean that anarchy will follow. A new kind of authority is based on information and on people exercising control through knowledge and competence.

Communication with the people who report to you is one means of increasing knowledge, developing skills, and enabling individuals and the organization to function together. Following the practices described in these chapters will inevitably result in more opportunities for learning and growth for the people in your unit. Suppose you adopt a problem solving mode rather than telling on implementation of procedures. Risks are involved, but the work unit may also function better as a result. And in the process people will learn how to use their experience to solve problems.

Career Goals

What positions do you see ahead and in what way does communication fit into your plan? For example, if you want to be a department head, more time will be spent in meetings, and providing explanations of organizational policy. Analysis of benefits from both a personal and organizational perspective is the next step in developing a personal communication plan. Use Table 7.3 to think through the benefits you wish to obtain. Then record them on the appropriate planning form.

TABLE 7.3   Summary of Benefits

	Giving Explanations	Performance Appraisal	Effective Meetings	Building Open Communications
Production or service results	_____	_____	_____	_____
Development of others	_____	_____	_____	_____
My career goals	_____	_____	_____	_____

---

[5] David Berlo, "Management—The Power Issue—Who's in Charge," speech given at Appalachian State University Conference on Communication within Organizations, Boone, North Carolina, August 19, 1977.

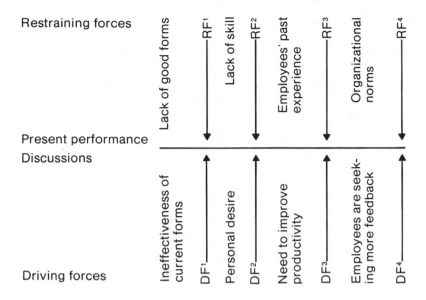

Figure 7.2   Force field analysis.

OBSTACLES

The ability to identify obstacles in advance is the key to the success of any plan. Understanding the barriers to change can help you to plan means to overcome them, have realistic expectations, and adapt to the situation. A conceptual scheme for the process of change has been developed by Kurt Lewin.[6] In Lewin's model change results from the release of tension. Tension is a state of readiness or preparation for action which arises from a need or a want.[7] In Lewin's analysis there are always tensions for maintaining the equilibrium (restraining forces) and tensions pushing for change (driving forces). (See Figure 7.2.) Take for example, your desire to improve performance discussions.

The driving forces are often parallel to the analysis of benefits, although not every benefit will have enough intensity to serve as a driving force. The restraining forces can come from two primary sources: within the organization and within yourself.

---

[6] Kenneth D. Benne and Max Birnbaum, "Principles of Changing," in *The Planning of Change*, Warren G. Bennis, Kenneth D. Benne, and Robert Chin, eds. (New York: Holt, Rinehart and Winston, 1969), p. 329.
[7] Alfred J. Marrow, *The Practical Theorist: The Life and Work of Kurt Lewin* (New York: Basic Books, 1977), p. 31.

Organizational Restraints

Organizational norms, the generally agreed expectations for behavior, are a powerful restraint to the forces of change.

In your organization the norm for managers may be that everyone comes in early and carries a briefcase home. No one told you this was expected. You observed the behavior in many managers, especially those moving up. Few organizations have the kinds of norms which allow people to question the purpose of meetings, and you will find it difficult to "go against the tide" when looking for the reasons for the meetings you attend. Or the norm may be to not tell the "troops" about organization changes until all decisions are made, which, of course, makes it difficult to openly discuss the concerns of your staff.

Organizational norms also make it difficult to transfer learning to the job. Experts in training have found that "trainees must feel free to apply what they learn and to change their behavior if they wish. When the organizational climate denies this freedom, subordinates are more likely to imitate their boss than to follow what they have learned in class."[8] And we might add, what they learned in a book!

Restraints Within Yourself

If you have ever tried to change any habit—smoking, not exercising—you know how difficult it is to change. Habits are deeply ingrained patterns of past experiences. Communications, perceiving experience and sharing it with others, is, in part, habitual.

If you frequently find yourself in the blaming mode of communication, it is likely that you have been doing it for a while, that you had a boss or parent or other authority figure who was also a blamer. You "learned" this behavior as a habit somewhere in your past experience. Changing a habit means some inconvenience, and you need to be prepared to be inconvenienced as you stop old habits—interrupting others—and substitute new—being an active listener.

We all strive to maintain a reasonable degree of equilibrium between ourselves and our environment. That is, we don't want to experience too much dissonance between our beliefs, values, attitudes and what is happening around us. Something is dissonant when two elements in our environment don't fit together.[9] For example, if you be-

---

[8] George Strauss and Leonard Sayles, *Personnel: The Human Problems of Management* (Englewood Cliffs, N.J.: Prentice-Hall, 1967), p. 570.
[9] Leon Festinger, *A Theory of Cognitive Dissonance* (Stanford Calif.: Stanford University Press, 1957), p. 13.

lieve that a manager should have all the anwers, you will find if difficult to say "I don't know" to someone who works for you. Your belief
and the reality simply don't fit together. Be prepared to experience
some dissonance as you undertake change; it will be disconcerting but
not insurmountable.

MEANS TO OVERCOME OBSTACLES

Once obstacles are identified, it is possible to plan means to overcome
them. Some typical obstacles managers encounter when they attempt
to change are:

> Unwillingness of employees to accept new behavior
> Restrictive organizational policies
> Own habits
> Lack of time
> Lack of feedback from others

Some of these obstacles lie outside the individual manager's capacity. Most will be difficult, but not impossible, to overcome. This is not
to say, however, that you should give up, though this may appear to be
the course of least resistance. One thing you have all learned by now in
your managerial careers is that communication problems do not go
away. Rather, they come back to haunt you in the form of crises,
missed deadlines, production errors, poor service to clients, and "people
problems." In a few situations they come back as equal rights cases, as
an employee seeks due process of law for redress of grievances. The
costs of litigation, settling minor claims, and class-action suits can add
greatly to an organization's operating costs.[10]

Taking on the entire organization, especially if it is a large one, is
on overwhelming task. Organizations are segmented into smaller units,
and you are responsible for one of them. Take responsibility for changing communication with the people who report directly to you, as this
is where you have the most influence. You also have a great deal of influence on *your* communication with peers and with the person to
whom you report.

The perceived unwillingness of employees to accept new behavior
on your part can be due to two factors: assumptions you are making,

---

[10] Arnold R. Deutsch, *The Human Resources Revolution: Communicate or Litigate*
(New York: McGraw-Hill, 1979), p. 171.

and the need for people to learn to trust new behavior. Some people will find it difficult to stay on track at a meeting, to accept performance feedback even when given in the most descriptive terms, to bring problems to your attention, to ask questions when they don't understand an explanation. For those who are truly unable to accept and respond to your communication, there is little you can do except acknowledge that you will lose some battles in the struggle to improve communication. However, this does not warrant the assumption that everyone will react this way. As you demonstrate sustained ability to engage in the more effective behaviors, many people will respond to you.

Another obstacle often cited is the lack of time. It takes time to plan for a clear explanation, for a performance review, for a meeting, for open communication. As with other matters in time management, it is a matter of priorities. Selecting your priorities is an important element in your communication plan. Allow yourself enough lead time to think about the behavior and about what you want to accomplish. Initially much of this will take extra time, but eventually the communication behaviors will become internalized and will be a natural part of your communication repertoire.

The lack of support from your own supervisor can be dealt with in a number of ways. First, don't try to assume responsibility for changing his or her behavior. Second, figure out why this person isn't giving you the support you need and try to respond to those reasons. Suppose your manager believes employees don't need to know about a new salary policy which you want to discuss at a meeting. Show the manager the benefits you think such a discussion will gain, especially those which will result in improved service or productivity or in fewer problems. Few managers can resist a plan which demonstrates a payoff for the work unit.

It may be frustrating to give an effective performance appraisal and then not to receive one, but you may be unable to have impact on your manager's behavior. (Some of the techniques, however, could help you to turn it around.) Open communication can be difficult to build if those above you are operating in a closed manner. Yet, if you select issues carefully and start on a small scale, you can improve the openness in your immediate environment.

It is impossible here to discuss all the ways to overcome obstacles which you may face as they will vary for each situation. The point is that you have more options available than you may realize. Before embarking on a communication improvement plan, consider what you can do to reduce the barriers and to assure success.

MONITOR AND EVALUATE YOUR PLAN

How will you know if you have achieved your goals? How can you keep yourself on track over time and in the face of pressure of the daily workload? Monitoring and evaluating the plan are the last step in communication improvement, and they are among the more difficult tasks.

Self-perception and self-insight play a vital role in this process. The specific behaviors listed in your plan will make it easier to monitor your progress. Each time you try a new behavior, allow time—even a few minutes—to "play back" what you did. Check off what you said against the stated goals and list of behaviors.

1. Did you ask open questions?
   Listen to the questions you asked.
2. How concrete was the performance feedback?
   What words did you use; were they descriptive?
3. Did the meeting stay on track?
   What did you say to help others to focus on the agenda?
4. How did you respond to "bad news"?
   Were you defensive or accepting?

Another technique is to periodically fill out the self-assessment forms without reference to previous forms until you are finished, and see if your results vary over time. What progress have you made? Identify what you need to do to meet the stated goals.

If your plan is part of a course or training program, meet with others in your group to see how each of you has fared. A group of people whom you trust and who have similar goals can be a great resource. Share your experiences, successes and failures, and help each other meet current goals.

Identify someone who is around you in your work situation and share your plan. Show this individual the guidelines for feedback so that he or she can describe your behavior. If you are not able to be this systematic, ask for feedback more informally. Don't say, "How did I do?" but rather, "How did you feel about the question I asked at the meeting?" or, "What is your view of how the new policy was explained?"

And, of course, look for results.

Policies and procedures should take less time to implement and should be carried out with fewer errors and misinterpretations.

Performance reviews should be somewhat easier as you are more competent, and employee performance should improve.

Meetings should be more productive and, in some cases, take less time. You ought to be able to identify times when you know a topic would have ended in misunderstanding but didn't because of your paraphrasing and summaries.

Are your people reporting bad news without fear of recrimination?

Are you aware of problems before they turn into crises?

Each of these is an indication that something has changed. We cannot say with certainty that your behavior was the only causal factor, but you will be able to identify differences in your relationships with others. This is when you take heart and reward yourself. Building in rewards for yourself is needed to reenforce and support your plan.

When the techniques for monitoring and evaluating behavior are recorded on the forms, your personal communication plan will be complete. Now it is up to you to implement it on a daily basis.

SUMMARY

The process for planning change in communication behavior outlined in this chapter is intended to maximize the results you can obtain from reading this book and doing the various exercises. Three months from now, six months or even a year from now, will your behavior have changed in the desired direction? Although filling out the communication planning forms is time-consuming, a written specific plan will focus on the changes you identified as needed in the self-assessment questionnaires.

A person who can communicate well while performing management functions will be recognized and rewarded by the organization. More importantly, you need to recognize, value, and reward the behavior yourself. Then, as you assume more responsibility for other managers and supervisors, you can coach, counsel, and support the kind of communication you desire.

You will be giving explanations, conducting performance reviews, going to meetings, and building open communication as you perform management functions. One day, perhaps imperceptibly, you will find yourself doing both without conscious effort and will, indeed, be a manager as communicator.

SELF-ASSESSMENT OF COMMUNICATION STYLE

Indicate the degree to which you do the following: (You might ask others to fill it out as well.)

	Very Little	Little	Some	Great	Very Great
1. Make judgments early in the conversation.					
2. Share my feelings with others.					
3. Talk about the issues.					
4. Have analyzed others' motives.					
5. Talk about the person.					
6. Use clear and precise language.					
7. Decide on the action before the conversation.					
8. Encourage the other person to discuss feelings.					
9. Am open for new information.					
10. Ask questions which seek agreement with me.					
11. Talk the majority of the time.					
12. Ask questions which get others to describe events.					
13. Talk half the time or less.					
14. Others defend their position to me.					

Scoring Sheet

Item No.	Score	
1	_____	
2		_____
3		_____
4	_____	
5	_____	
6		_____
7	_____	
8		_____
9		_____
10	_____	
11	_____	
12		_____
13		_____
14	_____	
Totals	_____	_____

Total column 1   _____
Total column 2   _____

very little = 1 point, little = 2 points, some = 3 points, great = 4 points, and very great = 5 points

SELF-ASSESSMENT OF MEETING SKILLS

Use the scale on the right to help assess your skill in carrying out each task or behavior for improving meetings. Your evaluation should be based on: (1) ability to perform the task or behavior, (2) knowing when each is appropriate or needed at a meeting, (3) willingness to actually engage in the behavior. The scale ranges from 1 (low) to 5 (high). After you have assessed each item listed, review your behavior and place a ✔ in the column to the far right indicating if you are satisfied or dissatisfied with your skill level.

Task Behaviors	1	2	3	4	5	Satisfied	Dissatisfied
1. *Initiating* goals and procedures to help a group organize their task.						___	___
2. *Seeking information*, getting others' opinions, information.						___	___
3. *Giving information*, providing own views of topic.						___	___
4. *Clarifying* terms which are ambiguous, *elaborating* on ideas.						___	___
5. *Summarizing* different points of view.						___	___
6. Checking for *consensuses*; determining areas of agreement or disagreement.						___	___
7. *Giving assignments* or directions for the next meeting.						___	___

	1	2	3	4	5	Satisfied	Dissatisfied

Maintenance Behaviors

1. *Encouraging* others by indicating acceptance.
2. *Harmonizing* by reducing tension; exploring personal differences between others.
3. *Managing differences* by exploring issues between self and others.
4. *Gatekeeping* to help everyone to participate, keeping the channels of communication open.
5. *Clarifying communication* by reflecting back what was said, asking others to restate what they heard before continuing.

Premeeting Planning

1. Discover goal of meeting.
2. Identify reasons for being asked.
3. Identify necessary info and act.
4. Identify own purpose for attending meeting.
5. If I call the meeting, go through necessary planning steps.

Postmeeting Planning

	1	2	3	4	5 Satisfied	Dissatisfied
1. Review goal achievement.						
2. Identify personal responsibilities.						
3. Evaluate my participation.						
4. Assess the use of time.						
5. Determine goal of next meeting.						

Problem Solving

1. Able to follow problem solving sequence to determine my contributions.						
2. Able to use problem solving sequence to set appropriate agenda when I call a meeting.						
3. Able to use problem solving sequence to help a group manage their time and information.						

SELF-ASSESSMENT OF GIVING EXPLANATIONS

Check the extent to which you think you do each of the following in giving explanations.

	Very Little	Little	Some	Great	Very Great
1. Frame a clear purpose for listeners.					
2. Consciously select the appropriate media.					
3. Put limits on the amount of material I want to cover.					
4. Use language with a common frame of reference.					
5. Provide transitions and summaries to help people follow me.					
6. Give appropriate qualifiers so action is clear.					
7. Encourage people to give me feedback.					

SELF-ASSESSMENT OF EFFECTIVENESS OF EXPLANATIONS

Check the extent to which each of the following usually occurs when I explain policies and procedures.

	Very Little	Little	Some	Great	Very Great
1. The purpose is clear.					
2. I know what you want me to do with the information.					
3. The explanation is in print when I need the spoken word.					
4. The explanation is oral when I need something in writing.					
5. Covers too much information at once.					
6. Gives so many qualifiers I'm not sure what you mean.					
7. Allows time for feedback and discussion.					
8. Encourages me to ask questions.					
9. Answers my questions clearly.					

POLICY CHECKLIST

To determine those policies which you should be particularly familiar with, check how often you need to explain them. There is also space to evaluate if your information is accurate, up to date and complete.

	Very Seldom	Seldom	Some- times	Often	Very Often	Accurate	Up to Date	Com- plete
1. Job-related procedures								
2. Technical manuals								
3. Budget requirements								
4. Change in work procedures								
5. Government regulations which affect our business								
6. New products or services								
7. Vacation/time off								
8. Salary								
9. Benefits								
10. Retirement								
11. Safety								
12. Training opportunities								
13. Performance expectations								
14. Career opportunities								
15. Probation/termination								

SELF-ASSESSMENT OF DISCUSSION SKILLS

Assess the level of your skills using the following scale:
1 = need work to acquire the skill; 2 = able to do—need to do more often; 3 = able to do—use effectively.

	1	2	3
1. Open the discussion effectively.	___	___	___
2. Able to define expected results.	___	___	___
3. Use concrete, descriptive language.	___	___	___
4. Back up value judgments with clear standards.	___	___	___
5. Use questions appropriately.	___	___	___
6. Responsive to other person's feelings.	___	___	___
7. Firm with negative feedback.	___	___	___
8. Listen to other person's point of view.	___	___	___
9. Not get "hooked" by negative responses.	___	___	___
10. Paraphrase other person's statements.	___	___	___

SELF-ASSESSMENT OF BUILDING OPEN COMMUNICATION

Check the extent to which you do each of the following:

	Very Little	Little	Some	Great	Very Great
1. I help others feel free to talk with me.					
2. I understand my employees' job problems.					
3. I encourage others to let me know when things are going wrong on the job.					
4. I make it easy for others to do their best work.					
5. I express confidence in my employees' ability to perform their job.					
6. I encourage others to bring new information to my attention, even when that new information may be bad news.					
7. Others feel that the things they tell me are usually important.					
8. I am willing to tolerate argument and to give a fair hearing to all points of view.					
9. I listen to the people who report to me when they state things that are bothering them.					
10. It's safe for my people to say what they are really thinking.					
11. People who report to me are frank and candid with me.					

12. My people can "sound off" about job frustrations to me. ___ ___ ___

13. My people can tell me about how they feel I am managing the work group. ___ ___ ___

14. My people are able to disagree with me. ___ ___ ___

15. People can communicate "bad news" to me without fear of retaliation on my part. ___ ___ ___

16. I believe I really understand the people who report to me. ___ ___ ___

17. My people think that they understand me. ___ ___ ___

18. The information I receive from my subordinates is reliable. ___ ___ ___

SOURCE: Adapted from Harry Dennis' Communication Climate Inventory.

PLANNING FORMS
COMMUNICATION PLANNING: GIVING EXPLANATIONS

Assessment of Skills	Change Goal	Skills/Knowledge	Appropriate Situation

Desired Benefits	Obstacles	Means To Overcome	Means To Monitor and Evaluate

COMMUNICATION PLANNING: PERFORMANCE APPRAISAL

Assessment of Skills	Change Goal	Skills/Knowledge	Appropriate Situation

Desired Benefits	Obstacles	Means To Overcome	Means To Monitor and Evaluate

COMMUNICATION PLANNING: EFFECTIVE MEETINGS

Assessment of Skills	Change Goal	Skills/Knowledge	Appropriate Situation

Desired Benefits	Obstacles	Means To Overcome	Means To Monitor and Evaluate

COMMUNICATION PLANNING: OPEN COMMUNICATION

Assessment of Skills	Change Goal	Skills/Knowledge	Appropriate Situation

Desired Benefits	Obstacles	Means To Overcome	Means To Monitor and Evaluate

APPENDIXES

The appendixes include examples of organizational policies which aid the manager's communication. The corporate policies are used with permission of the organizations.

The Dennis Communication Climate Inventory is an example of a questionnaire which could be used to describe communication within a work unit.

APPENDIX A
PERFORMANCE APPRAISAL
POLICY: MICHIGAN
CREDIT UNION LEAGUE

The policy of the Michigan Credit Union League and affiliates is to recognize and reward performance and thereby to aid individual employees in meeting job expectations and fulfilling personal career goals. To carry out this policy, all employees will participate in discussions regarding their performance.

The Michigan Credit Union League and affiliates consists of several organizations fulfilling somewhat different missions. We are, however, one organization with the common goal of providing service to credit unions and their members. Thus, employees performance within the Michigan Credit Union League and afflliates should be evaluated in a consistent and uniform manner.

GOALS OF PERFORMANCE APPRAISAL PROGRAM

The Performance Appraisal Program is intended to achieve the following objectives:

> Employees will be better able to perform their jobs when they know what is expected of them.
>
> Individual performance and unit productivity will be improved through mutually agreed upon goals.
>
> Reliable data will be available for decisions concerning merit increases, promotions, transfers, and dismissals.

The organization will be improved by identifying people with promotion potential and pinpointing developmental needs.

Employees will become aware of opportunities to influence their own careers and work goals.

FREQUENCY AND TIMING

Performance appraisals will be held for every employee at least twice a year. More frequent discussions will be held for new employees, employees new on a job, and employees identified as below performance standards. In most cases these appraisals will occur every three months. Supervisors will have the discretion to appraise performance more often, if they deem necessary, for recognition of significant improvement.

To help assure fairness and consistency, the Performance Appraisal Summary will be reviewed by the next level of management, above the evaluating supervisor or manager. In most situations the management review will occur before discussion with the employee.

Salary reviews, as in the past, will be conducted at least annually. While it is recognized that performance appraisal and salary are related, the salary review and appropriate recommendation will be separate from the performance appraisal discussion. Performance appraisal discussions will be scheduled within three months prior to a salary review.

RESPONSIBILITY FOR PERFORMANCE APPRAISAL

Management at all levels is responsible for following a reasonable schedule of interviews and will be held accountable for administration of this policy.

Employees will have the opportunity to review their supervisor's evaluation during the discussion, to write individual comments, and to sign the form. Forms will be kept in the personnel files.

CLIMATE FOR DISCUSSION

To achieve the goals of this policy, a give and take discussion is needed. An open climate, where ideas, feelings, problems, and aspirations are freely exchanged, does not come with one discussion. In building this climate, the program includes forms to be used by both employees and supervisors in preparing for the appraisal discussion. The program emphasizes objective factors and results of job performance and will be based upon performance standards as they are established.

TRAINING

To aid in implementation of the policy, an ongoing mandatory training program will be conducted to help those at every level who administer the policy. This training will explain the policy and develop needed communication skills.

APPENDIX B
PRIVACY POLICY:
EQUITABLE LIFE
ASSURANCE SOCIETY

In recognition of the rights of all individuals, it will be our policy and practice to so conduct our business as to protect the rights of privacy of all those customers, agents, and employees associated with us. We shall do this in ways that are reasonable and consistent with good business practices, with the rights of individuals as our ultimate guideline.

In the ongoing pursuit of this principle, we shall:

1. Request and use only that personal information which is pertinent to the effective conduct of business;
2. Consider personal information collected and maintained to be of a confidential nature, recognizing our responsibility to provide adequate safeguards to maintain that confidentiality;
3. Refuse to make available, without the knowledge of the individual, personal information outside The Equitable or its subsidiaries, except to provide routine service or as required by law;
4. Make available to employees and agents, upon proper request, any information we maintain on them, recognizing our obligation to protect the privacy of the source of the information;
5. Make available to policyowners and applicants, upon proper request, any information we maintain on them, recognizing our obligation to protect the privacy of the source of the information, and in the case of medical information, supplying that through the individual's physician;
6. Correct or delete any information found to be inaccurate, thus recognizing the importance of using timely and accurate infor-

mation so that action adverse to an individual is not based on erroneous data;

7. Expect all employees and agents to conform to our well-established ethical standards as to the confidentiality of personal information held by The Equitable.

APPENDIX C
TRW EMPLOYEE
COMMUNICATIONS PRINCIPLES
AND GUIDELINES

This statement underscores the importance TRW places on communications throughout the organization worldwide. It reaffirms the value of open and frank communications between people at all levels and in all parts of the company as an essential contributor to personal and organizational growth and progress. It establishes basic principles of communications designed to assist and encourage all parts of TRW to reach and maintain consistent excellence in employee communications performance. The statement contains a series of guidelines for managers but deliberately does not prescribe the specific content of employee communication plans, leaving instead those decisions to the discretion of local management.

EMPLOYEE COMMUNICATIONS PRINCIPLES

Primary responsibility for communications rests with responsible managers at individual TRW organizational units at all levels—plants, divisions, groups, corporate staff, and the CEO.

Communications to and from each employee and the immediate supervisor is particularly important and is the most crucial communications link in developing an ongoing, open system of listening, talking, and acting that affects attitudes and productivity.

Employee communications is a component of the company's integrated communications function which also includes advertising and public relations, government relations, community relations, and investor relations.

Other key principles underlie the value of downward, upward, and lateral communications.

DOWNWARD COMMUNICATIONS PRINCIPLES

TRW managers need to recognize that:

TRW employees at all levels need and deserve to know about company developments that affect their productivity, opportunity, individual growth, job security, feelings of self-worth, and quality of work life.

TRW communications to employees need to be frank and open in discussing objectives, problems, difficulties, and opportunities.

TRW employees at all levels need to know in varying degrees what the company's opportunities, scope of interests, and problems are so they may: (a) contribute to the development of company goals and objectives; (b) help the company achieve goals and objectives that otherwise may not be attained.

Upward Communications Principles

TRW managers need to know, take seriously, and be responsive to what employees at all levels:

Think and feel about the company and their jobs.

See as problems.

Have as suggestions about the business and about programs the company is trying to carry out.

Like about the company and their work.

Don't like about the company and their work.

Lateral Communications Principles

TRW managers need to:

Appreciate and manage the interdependence within their organizational units—e.g., staff/line, sales/manufacturing/engineering—and regard effective communications as a means to resolve conflicts and build cooperation between functions.

Understand and identify with the goals and objectives of higher levels of the organization, e.g., plant managers with division goals, group vice presidents with overall company goals.

Expect continued priority on delegation of responsibility, including responsibility for cooperation and support of other line and staff units needed to achieve overall company objectives.

GUIDELINES FOR PLANTS, DIVISIONS, SUBSIDIARIES

A good employee communications program at the plant, division, subsidiary level generally includes the following features· or their equivalent:

Downward Communications

An employee newspaper or newsletter issued at least four times a year reporting on important business developments of interest and concern to all employees and on significant employee activities and achievements.

Some form of face-to-face meetings about goals and objectives, forecasts, problems, and opportunities held at least once a year, with employees.

Some form of written communications on issues such as goals and objectives, forecasts, problems, and opportunities sent to all employees at least once a year.

Some form of staff meetings developed and some form of transfer of information from staff meetings at all levels down through the organization with particular emphasis on getting current information to first-line supervision on a regular basis.

Upward Communications

A continual organization diagnosis and improvement program developed and implemented which uses various data collection techniques—such as the 1-in-5 small group interview process and written surveys—reports back to all employees the data learned in the diagnosis, undertakes some form of concrete action on the data learned, and evaluates results.

Lateral Communications

Open communication systems developed among functions designed to raise problems and work solutions collaboratively and to place particular emphasis on the open sharing of appropriate information within and between management teams at all levels. Tech-

niques such as management meetings, team building, interfunc-
tional problem identification sessions, and skip level meetings
are used.

Appropriate links developed to other parts of TRW to share information and identify resources where justified by mutual interests such as common geographic regions, similar markets, technology, or manufacturing processes.

GUIDELINES FOR GROUP AND EXECUTIVE VICE PRESIDENTS

A good employee communications program at the group vice president
and executive vice president levels generally includes the following
features or their equivalent:

Downward Communications

Some form of written communications on goals and objectives,
forecasts, problems, and opportunities issued to key plant and division managers and their staffs within their group at least once
a year.

Periodic participation in some form of plant and divison staff
meetings and/or employee meetings within their group.

Upward Communications

A continual organization diagnosis and improvement program in-
volving their key managers developed and implemented which
uses various data collection techniques—written surveys, informal skip level sensing sessions—reports back to all managers the
data learned in the diagnosis, undertakes some form of concrete
action on the data learned, and evaluates results.

Lateral Communications

A management conference of their key managers held at least
once every two years.

Permanent working groups within their functions and temporary
working groups as needed to work specific projects developed by
group staff department heads.

At least one division in groups other than their own visited by executive vice presidents each year.

GUIDELINES FOR CORPORATE STAFF AND THE CEO

A good employee communications program at the corporate staff and CEO levels generally includes the following features or their equivalent:

Downward Communications

Some form of communications on goals and objectives, public policy positions, forecasts, problems, and opportunities of overall company interest issued by the CEO to TRW managers down to and including plant managers at least once a year. It is expected that managers receiving this information will distribute it broadly throughout their organizations.

Some form of communications on goals and objectives, public policy positions, problems, and opportunities relating to their function issued by corporate staff department heads to TRW managers down to and including plant managers at least once a year.

Two to three plants and divisions visited by CEO members and corporate staff department heads each year.

Upward Communications

At least two informal skip level sensing meetings with key managers held by the CEO once a year.

At least one informal skip level sensing meeting with managers in function held by each corporate staff department head each year.

Lateral Communications

A pattern of meetings held by the CEO at which key TRW managers see current financial results, have the opportunity to hear about major plans, projects, and priorities within TRW and are exposed to broad corporatewide interests and concerns.

Group management conferences attended by the CEO and corporate staff department heads where practical and appropriate.

Permanent companywide working groups within their functions and temporary working groups as needed to work specific projects developed by corporate staff department heads.

APPENDIX D
DENNIS COMMUNICATION
CLIMATE INVENTORY

Factor I (Superior/Subordinate Communication)

_____ Your superior makes you feel free to talk with him/her.

_____ Your superior really understands your job problems.

_____ Your superior encourages you to let him/her know when things are going wrong on the job.

_____ Your superior makes it easy for you to do your best work.

_____ Your superior expresses his/her confidence with your ability to perform the job.

_____ Your superior encourages you to bring new information to his/her attention, even when that new information may be bad news.

_____ Your superior makes you feel that things you tell him/her are really important.

_____ Your superior is willing to tolerate arguments and to give a fair hearing to all points of view.

_____ Your superior has your best interests in mind when he/she talks to his/her bosses.

_____ Your superior is a really competent, expert manager.

_____ Your superior listens to you when you tell him/her about things that are bothering you.

_____ It is safe to say what you are really thinking to your superior.

_____ Your superior is frank and candid with you.

_____ You can "sound off" about job frustrations to your superior.

_____ You can tell your superior about the way you feel he/she manages your work group.

_____   You are free to tell your superior that you disagree with him/her.

_____   You think you are safe in communicating "bad news" to your superior without fear of any retaliation on his/her part.

_____   You think that your superior believes that he/she really understands you.

_____   You believe that your superior thinks that you understand _him/her_.

_____   Your superior really understands you.

_____   You really understand your superior.

Factor II (Quality of Information)

_____   You think that people in this organization say what they mean and mean what they say.

_____   People in top management say what they mean and mean what they say.

_____   People in this organization are encouraged to be really open and candid with each other.

_____   People in this organization freely exchange information and opinions.

_____   You are kept informed about how well organizational goals or objectives are being met.

_____   Your organization succeeds in rewarding and praising good performance.

_____   Top management is providing you with the kinds of information you really want and need.

_____   You are receiving information from those sources (for example, from superiors, department meetings, co-workers, newsletters) that you prefer.

_____   You are pleased with management's efforts to keep employees up-to-date on recent developments that relate to the organization's welfare—such as success in competition, profitability, future growth plans, etc.

_____   You are notified in advance of changes that affect your job.

_____   You are satisfied with explanations you get from top management about why things are done as they are.

_____   Your job requirements are specified in clear language.

Factor III (Superior Openness/Candor)

_____   You believe your subordinates are really frank and candid with you.

_____   You believe your colleagues (co-workers) are really frank and candid with you.

_____   You think your subordinates are feeling free to "sound off" to you about things that bother them.

_____   You believe that you really understand your subordinates' problems.

_____   You believe that your subordinates think that *you* really understand *their* problems.

Factor IV (Upward Communication Opportunity)

_____   Your opinions make a difference in the day-to-day decisions that affect your job.

_____   Your superior lets you participate in the planning of your own work.

_____   Members of your work group are able to establish their own goals and objectives.

_____   You believe your views have real influence in your organization.

_____   You can expect that recommendations you make will be heard and seriously considered.

Factor V (Reliability of Information)

_____   You think that information received from your subordinates is really reliable.

_____   You think that information received from your colleagues (co-workers) is reliable.

INDEX